# THE GRAND PORTAGE STORY

# THE GRAND PORTAGE STORY

## Carolyn Gilman

With research by Alan R. Woolworth

9208

Minnesota Historical Society Press • St. Paul

*This book was produced as a joint project of Grand Portage National Monument and the Minnesota Historical Society. Major funding was provided by the National Park Service, and additional funds came from contributions to the Society made by numerous individuals and organizations in support of Grand Portage history.*

**Minnesota Historical Society Press**
**St. Paul 55101**

Manufactured in Singapore
10  9  8  7  6  5  4  3  2  1

This publication is printed on a coated paper manufactured on an acid-free base to ensure its long life.

**Library of Congress Cataloging-in-Publication Data**

Gilman, Carolyn, 1954–
    The Grand Portage story / Carolyn Gilman with research by Alan R. Woolworth.
                        p.    cm.
    Includes bibliographical references (p.    ) and index.
    ISBN 0-87351-270-7 (paper : acid-free)
    1. Grand Portage Region (Minn.)—History.  2. Grand Portage National Monument (Minn.)—History.  I. Woolworth, Alan R. (Alan Roland), 1924– . II. Title.
F614.G7G55  1992
977.6'75—dc20                                            91-41804

# Contents

# Foreword

A cedar picket stockade on the shore of Lake Superior is the first sight that draws a visitor's attention at Grand Portage National Monument. It surrounds a reconstruction of the depot that stood there in the late 1700s during the heyday of the North American fur trade. But the greatest historic legacy at this place is the 8.5-mile portage route winding from the stockade through the forest to join the Pigeon River above the falls and rapids that make the river's lower 22 miles impassable. This trail is the *Kitchi Onigaming* or Grand Portage, the vital link that Indians and voyageurs followed when traveling between the lake and the interior.

The Grand Portage area has been a crossroads of cultures for hundreds of years. It has been a site of continuous Indian settlement, with one group displacing another at times of war or shifts in population. It hosted a complex trading alliance between Indians and Europeans when it served as the geographical center of a vast commercial network. People who lived there or merely traveled through left invaluable records of the personalities and events that characterized Grand Portage at different times.

Recognizing the importance of this story, the National Park Service approached the Minnesota Historical Society for help in producing a comprehensive handbook on the site. For several decades the Society and the National Park Service sponsored archaeological work on the fur trade era at Grand Portage, and the reference collections at the Society include a rich variety of material on Indian history and the fur trade. Alan R. Woolworth, formerly chief archaeologist and now a research fellow on the staff of the Minnesota Historical Society, generously provided information from files that he assembled during eight summers of work at Grand Portage. Carolyn Gilman, who has conducted extensive research into the fur trade and into contact between Indian and non-Indian cultures, carried out fur-

ther research and wrote the narrative. The National Park Service provided funds to help support the project.

Others who merit thanks for their help in this effort include Jennifer S.
H. Brown, Jean Morrison, Ellen B. Olson, Margaret Plummer-Steen, Curtis L. Roy, and Erwin N. Thompson. Site interpreters Don Carney and
Karen Evens at the National Monument and Bill Corcoran and Rick Novit-
sky at the Grand Portage Reservation provided advice and assistance. Par-
ticipating staff members at the Society included Ruth Bauer, Patricia Har-
pole, Steven Nielsen, and Alissa Rosenberg of the Reference Department;
Margaret Robertson of the Acquisitions and Curatorial Department; Charles
O. Diesen of Museum Collections; and Elaine H. Carte, Anne R. Kaplan,
Alan Ominsky, Ann Regan, Sarah P. Rubinstein, Deborah Swanson, and
Marilyn F. Ziebarth of the MHS Press.

We hope that this book will give readers a glimpse into the lives and traditions of the people who shaped the history of Grand Portage.

Grand Portage National Monument                    DEAN C. EINWALTER

# CHAPTER ONE

# The Boundary of East and West

The cars whish by on Highway 61, doing the Duluth-to-Thunder Bay run in speeded-up, twentieth-century time. The asphalt swoops up the side of Mount Josephine and treats drivers to a spectacular view down the North Shore of Lake Superior, a standing battle line of rock and spray. Then they're at the Canadian border. The hamlet of Grand Portage, nestled down on the coast, is invisible except for the impersonal green and white of a highway sign.

Two hundred years ago others traveled past this place, but their routes ran east-west, not north-south, and they came to different boundaries. Then, Grand Portage was one of the busiest spots west of the Appalachians. It was the most remote in a chain of rendezvous and transfer points for the industry that first put a European mark on the west: the fur trade. For most, Grand Portage wasn't journey's end; it was a place to pass on the way to somewhere else. But as with watersheds and thresholds, the act of passing Grand Portage was sometimes more important than arriving at the final destination.

Grand Portage was a crossroads where two transportation systems and two contrasting cultures met. Furs trapped and cleaned by Indian people all across the half-continent between Lake Superior and the Rocky Mountains were channeled through this spot. At the lakeshore the furs changed places with goods imported from around the world for Indian use. By the 1780s Grand Portage was headquarters of the famous North West Company, a commercial network that stretched from London to Oregon and the Arctic. But businesses, less permanent than peoples, came and went. Nations shouldered each other aside for a while, and in the end the spot was left in the care of its longest inhabitants, the Ojibway Indians. Today, it is still an Indian place.

A modern visitor to Grand Portage is surrounded by boundaries. There is, of course, the conspicuous one five miles to the north—the international boundary with the guards and drug-sniffing dogs. But it is neither the oldest nor the deepest. Long before nations, there were the boundaries of water and rock, of known and unknown, of east and west, of peoples. They are all still here, like overlapping wrinkles.

The oldest boundary at Grand Portage is very old indeed. The hills are made from some of the most ancient rock on earth. It was formed during the Precambrian era, when the only life was single-celled organisms like algae and bacteria. About 1,200 million years ago this part of the North American continent began to split apart in a huge crack that stretches down the North Shore of Lake Superior, through the St. Croix River valley, and as far south as Kansas. Basaltic lava welled up, then for some reason stopped. A scar of volcanic rock was left through what is now one of the most geologically stable areas in the world. At Grand Portage, the basalt forms huge dikes or linear hills running northeast to southwest, stretch marks along what might have been the edge of a continent. It is these dikes that form the falls on the Pigeon River, and through them the portage trail must thread.[1]

Hat Point on the coast of Lake Superior as seen on a late September morning

The North Shore of Lake Superior is the southern edge of the Canadian Shield—a vast country of rock scraped clean by glaciers. It offers little to support humans but is rich in one thing—waterways. Starting at Grand Portage with a canoe and a lot of energy, a person could reach the Atlantic, the Pacific, the Gulf of Mexico, Hudson Bay, or the Arctic Ocean without a single portage much longer than the Grand Portage itself.

The next oldest boundary can't be found on any map. It is everywhere: the once-permeable boundary between the spirit world and the world of humans. The oldest inhabitants of this land were mysterious beings known to us only through Ojibway testimony. There were the *maymaygwaysiwuk*, elusive little people who lived underwater and paddled stone canoes; the *michipichou*, or malevolent underwater lynx; the wise thunderbirds, who made stone nests on the cloudy heights; and many more. The shores of Lake Superior were once studded with offering rocks to these beings. Both Indians and whites left gifts on these natural altars where other worlds meshed with ours. One such spot still exists at Grand Portage. On the

A *maymaygwaysiwuk* as depicted by Ojibway artist Norval Morriseau

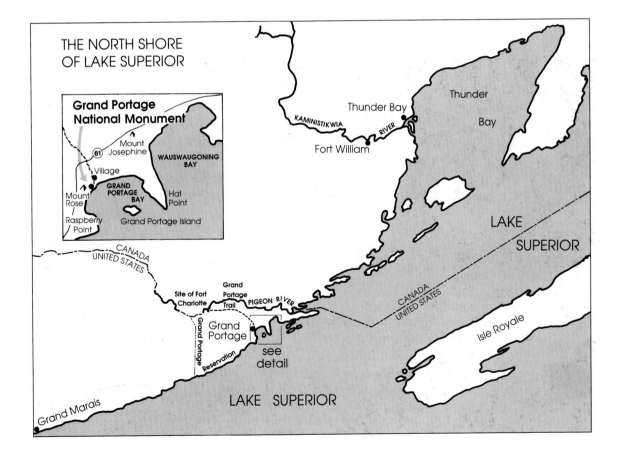

THE NORTH SHORE OF LAKE SUPERIOR

Grand Portage National Monument

Mount Josephine

61

Village

WAUSWAUGONING BAY

GRAND PORTAGE BAY

Mount Rose

Hat Point

Raspberry Point

Grand Portage Island

CANADA UNITED STATES

Thunder Bay

KAMINISTIKWIA

RIVER

Fort William

Thunder Bay

LAKE SUPERIOR

CANADA UNITED STATES

Site of Fort Charlotte

Grand Portage Trail

PIGEON RIVER

Grand Portage

Grand Portage Reservation

see detail

Isle Royale

Grand Marais

LAKE SUPERIOR

north side of Hat Point, on a stone ledge, is a twisted cedar—the *Manito Geezhigaynce,* or little spirit cedar tree. Once, it was inhabited by a being that appeared to humans in the shape of a huge eagle. Travelers on the cold, angry inland ocean seldom failed to stop and leave it a gift and a prayer. Today, the spirit beings of Lake Superior have mostly gone. But once they were powers as awesome and terrible as the lake itself.[2]

To the first Europeans who ventured into this land, Grand Portage became another sort of boundary: between the known and unknown. These men were bent on a mission of "discovery"—viewing the land through a new set of symbols, a new frame of reference. They wanted to know what *use* the land was to them. So they asked about travel routes and trade. The Great Lakes formed an unparalleled highway into the center of the continent. But beyond them lay the barrier of the Canadian Shield and of new, strange peoples. Only three paths crossed the shield barrier—the southernmost by the St. Louis River, which was soon closed off by war; the northernmost by the Kaministikwia River, which was long and shallow; and, in the middle, the Pigeon River route, which led by an almost uninterrupted chain of lakes and rivers clear to Lake Winnipeg and the plains. It is the main water route west of Lake Superior, and its only major obstruction is near the lake, where the Pigeon plunges through basalt chasms in a foaming chain of cataracts. To bypass it, Indian travelers had marked out an eight-and-a-half-mile overland path they called *Kitchi Onigaming*— in French, Grand Portage.

As European trade with the Indians grew over the years, supply depots and bases sprang up in the west. One was at Detroit, where Lakes Huron and Erie meet; one was at Michilimackinac, where Lakes Michigan and Huron meet. Grand Portage was the westernmost point where goods could be delivered from the east by ship, and so it also became a hub of commerce. It was the boundary of east and west in those days, where the colonial mercantilism of Europe met a commercial system ruled by Indian values—and adapted. Here, whites learned the ways of a culture oriented not toward profit so much as prestige, not toward resource exploitation but equilibrium.

Grand Portage's importance as a meeting place of peoples later was destroyed by another boundary: a boundary of nations, the United States and Canada. Wars and treaties in places the local people had never heard of erected an invisible barrier along the Pigeon River, slicing the Ojibway land in two. The North West Company, owned by British Canadians, was forced to abandon its headquarters at Grand Portage in 1803 and move forty miles north to Fort William on the Kaministikwia. There, using the profits made at Grand Portage, the company built another headquarters that eclipsed the old one in grandeur.

Other boundaries soon crowded close upon the Ojibway who remained. In 1854 they gave up much of the land they once used, from Grand Marais to Fort William, from Lake Superior to Rainy Lake. A reservation line was drawn around them and some 51,840 acres of their land.[3] But in the 1880s the government initiated a program to erase all boundaries between Indians and whites, to turn everyone into melting-pot Americans. The reservation was carved up into 160-acre lots surrounded by private property lines, and white settlers moved in to buy up much of the land. There was almost no space left to be Indian.

Today, much of Grand Portage Reservation's land has returned to Indian hands, and the reservation boundaries have been reasserted from within. Older cultural boundaries also are growing stronger. Slowly the world is coming to realize that boundaries can be valuable things. It is along the edges that our cultures are most creative. Where people can see what lies outside, change and innovation happen. And the places of overlap can be the most interesting of all.

From 1730 to 1805, Grand Portage was an emporium of goods and cultures as varied as any in the world. Like any place where peoples meet, it had a flavor all its own. Let's step back in imagination to a July day in the 1790s, when Grand Portage was in its heyday as a fur traders' rendezvous.

We'll spirit ourselves to the top of Mount Rose, the most prominent landmark on Grand Portage Bay. It is sunrise. To the south, the vast inland sea of Lake Superior is a plain of pewter meeting the horizon. Grand Portage Bay forms a half-circle indentation in the lakeshore, framed by Pointe aux Chapeaux (Hat Point) to the northeast and Pointe à la Framboise (Raspberry Point) to the southwest. Grand Portage Island lies in the jaws of the bay. This morning the bay and the beachline are hidden by a layer of chilly gray mist. Inland to the north, ridge upon ridge of dark green hills rise, covered with spruce, fir, and white pine.

It is very quiet. There's a smell of woodsmoke in the air, for already plumes rise from the kitchen chimney within the stockade below and from a campfire in the Indian village nearby. A dog barks; a woman hushes him. Now someone is heading toward the barn, pail banging against his leg, to milk the cows. Out on the bay the sailing ship *Otter* is riding at anchor. You can hear the sound, magnified by the mist, as someone starts to wash the deck. The crew is getting ready to ballast her for another run back to Sault Ste. Marie.

As the mist thins, you can see the layout of the buildings below. Close by, nestled under the hill at the mouth of a creek, is the palisaded outline of the North West Company's post, crowded with shingle-roofed buildings. Inland from it, along both sides of the creek, is a little village of white

The High Falls of the
Pigeon River, about a
mile from Lake Superior

tents—the campsite of the *gens du nord*, or northmen, the canoemen who have transported furs here from the company's scattered posts across the west. Across the creek, near the lakeshore, lies the camp of the *mangeurs de lard*, or pork eaters, who paddled here from the east in freight canoes loaded with goods from Montreal. The men in both camps are *voyageurs* (travelers)—the manual laborers who carry the goods of the fur trade by boat or on their backs. Up to a thousand people pass through each summer during the 1790s, but there are rarely more than four or five hundred here at a time. Beyond the camps the lakeshore is cleared and fenced. Eastward down the beach lies a second post—a small, ramshackle affair only occupied in summer—that sells goods to the canoemen. On the land beyond the little fort competing companies from time to time put up buildings. Inland from the camps on a ridge is a cemetery full of wooden crosses and Ojibway grave markers. To the north runs the portage trail, following the creek. It threads through a gap in the hills and meets the Pigeon River at Fort Charlotte eight and a half miles to the northwest.[4]

Descending Mount Rose, we find the depot already astir. The place is segregated by social class, language, ethnicity, and religion. The first enclave we come upon is the camp of the northmen, where the dialect is a French-

The reconstructed North West Company depot on Grand Portage Bay as seen from Mount Rose; Hat Point lies in the distance.

Indian patois and the religion an Indian-influenced Catholicism. To the Anglo-Gaelic elite, these are men "of the lowest class." Their white tents of Russia sheeting seemed to a visitor in 1793 to be "pitched at random, the people of each [inland] post having a camp by themselves." The portage trail runs through the cluster of tents. Although most of the men are still sleeping off a binge from last night, some of the Indian and mixed-blood wives who have come along are already up and working. Many of the *gens du nord* are family men whose homes are in the west.[5]

There are no surviving descriptions of the Grand Portage voyageurs' camp, but it must have looked much like others. "We had to sit cross-leg, tailor fashion, round our dish, when at meals," said one traveler. "We kindled a fire *out-doors* & boiled our Tea Kettle, & the men hung their Tea Kettles on the 'tripied' to make their Soupe. Our Kitchen furniture was a Tea Kettle, a tin Kettle to cook in, a frying pan; tinned plates."[6]

Some of the women are cooking breakfast. When the northmen first arrived, the company regaled them with unaccustomed luxuries: bread, pork, butter, liquor, and tobacco. Since then, they have had to make do with the standard daily ration—"a Quart of Lyed Indian Corn or maize, and one ounce of Greece." The "Lyed Indian Corn" (we would call it hominy grits) is shipped in from Detroit, its main advantage being that it is "the cheapest provision that can be procured." Boiled into a thick pudding, this food was once declared by one of the men in charge (who didn't have to eat it) "an wholesome, palatable food, and easy of digestion." It is, however, "by no means relished by the people, as this was *all* they had." One trader concluded that the difficulty of reconciling "any other men, than Canadians, to this fare, seems to secure to them . . . the monopoly of the fur-trade."[7]

While here the northmen will collect their annual salary, pay their debts to the company, and renew any expiring contracts if they wish to stay in the west. Some have to visit the doctor. They also need to collect the equipment the company allows them each year: two blankets, two shirts, two pairs of trousers, and tobacco.[8]

Crossing the creek eastward by a natural ford in the middle of the northmen's camp, we come to the pork eaters' side. To judge by one description, the two camps form a contrast: while the northmen's is tidy, the pork eaters' is filthy. There is "a sort of warfare" between the two camps, for the northmen consider themselves an elite, by virtue of experience, and let the others know it. It doesn't help that the men are all "indulging themselves in the free use of liquor, and quarrelling with each other" so much that it is "a necessary precaution for the Traders at the Grand Portage to keep their men apart as much as possible." Doubtless the creek cools off many a hot temper.[9] Instead of tents, "the more frugal pork-eater lodges beneath his canoe." Some of these men are Iroquois, but most are farmers from the small French-Canadian villages around Montreal. Though they're part-timers, on the trip to Grand Portage they adopt a voyageur subculture complete with rituals and songs. (Not the sanitized versions sold in gift shops today; the words of the more authentic songs were so obscene that one shocked historian suppressed them as "unfit for publication.") As we near, we find the pork eaters to be "sinister-looking, long-haired men, in blanket coats, and ostrich feathers in their hats, smoking and cooking, and feeding the fires." They all smell of sweat and tobacco. They are dressed in "a cloth, passed about the middle; a shirt, hanging loose; a molton, or blanket coat; and a large, red, milled worsted cap" or a handkerchief wrapped around the head. Aside from moccasins, which all the lower classes wear, you see very few leather clothes here. Cloth is one of the main commodities of the fur trade, and a salesman who doesn't use his own goods is a poor advertisement. Besides, in their jobs the voyageurs are constantly getting wet, and leather gets clammy and stiff.[10]

These men are not enjoying the leisure that reigns in the northmen's camp. They are the human beasts of burden who have to transport all the goods and furs across the eight-and-one-half-mile portage. Each man, by contract, has eight "pieces" (bales, chests, kegs) weighing ninety pounds each to carry across and four bales of furs to bring back. And if there are still goods left, the men can earn a Spanish dollar for each additional package. They are also obliged to give six days of manual labor—probably felling and hewing trees, sawing boards, putting up buildings, fetching

During a 1989 reenactment of the voyageurs' journey, David S. Wiggins carried two bales down to the Granite River at the end of Blueberry Portage.

firewood, cutting hay, and other tasks much like those on their farms at home. Some of them will be chosen to man a brigade going on to a rendezvous farther west at Rainy Lake, where they will meet the canoes from Athabasca, which cannot make it to Grand Portage and back in a single season. Some pork eaters will sign on as winterers, switching places with northmen whose contracts have expired.[11]

A side trip over to the little fort down the shore from the pork eaters' camp brings us to a shop and canteen operated with a semblance of independence by a man named Joseph Lecuyer. In reality, though, it's a company store. Lecuyer is outfitted by, and splits the profits with, the North West Company. Here the men can buy capotes, jackets, breeches, and other dry goods. If they are tired of hominy they can splurge on better fare, and of course there is wine and rum. Lecuyer's prices would shock anyone from the east. A cotton shirt worth eight francs or less in Montreal costs twelve here, but it's still cheaper than buying things at the wintering posts. Most of the customers are northmen, who have both the need and the money for extras. But no one has cash. They pay Lecuyer in two currencies: either *pactons* (coarse furs or hides the company lets them bring down from the west) or *bons* (vouchers for wages from the company).[12]

Sometimes Lecuyer gets more colorful customers—small traders who call themselves *gens libres* or freemen because they're not *engagés* of any company. Many are mixed-bloods who trade with their mothers' tribes. They bring their furs down to sell to the North West Company. Sometimes there are enough to hold an auction.[13]

The weather has changed, as it often does here. Now there is a brisk, chilly breeze, and the lake is a dazzling field of glitter under the windy blue sky. As we stroll down to the beach, disturbing a crew of raucous gulls feeding on discarded fish guts, we see two log wharfs where the company's four skiffs are tied up. Some are rowboats and some are probably sailing dinghies, used for shuttling cargo from the sailing ship to shore. The bay here is so shallow that the ship can't come in to the wharf while fully laden, so it spends most of the time anchored out in the lee of the island.[14]

There is a shout. One of the men nearby is gesturing out toward Pointe aux Chapeaux. Around the point comes a brigade of huge Montreal canoes, paddles flashing in the sun. One canoe is flying a Union Jack, a signal that one of the company's agents from Montreal is aboard. Spectators line the beach. Some men issue from the post with muskets. As the canoes come near, they fire off a *feu de joie* to honor the new arrivals. The canoe crew answers by bellowing out a French song. The gentlemen passengers are dressed stylishly—you can be sure they stopped nearby last night to shave, wash, and change clothes.[15]

The gentlemen's canoe pulls up at the wharf, but most of the others must land on the beach—a tricky maneuver, for they are too fragile to touch ground. It is done this way: "The first [canoe] makes a dash at the beach. Just as the last wave is carrying the canoe on dry ground, all her men jump out at once and support her; while her gentlemen or clerks hurry out her lading. During this time the other canoes are, if possible, heading out into the lake; but now one approaches, and is seized by the crew of the canoe first beached, who meet her up to the middle in water, and who, assisted by her own people, [unload the cargo and] lift her up high and dry." Lifting the empty vessel takes at least six men, who "reversed the canoe and in an instant shouldered it, which required great expertness, as any slip or accident would have destroyed the vessel, beyond the power of repairing."[16]

These are the biggest birch-bark canoes you're ever likely to see. Thirty-six feet long, six feet wide at the middle, the Montreal canoe looks like a "flimsy vessel" but can carry four tons. Each one has a crew of eight to ten men. As they are unloaded we can see what the canoes hold. First there are the sixty pieces—chests, kegs, and bales wrapped in water-repellent canvas. Then the canoe equipment: two oilcloths, a mast and sail (yes, they can sail with a tailwind), an ax, a kettle, a towing line, a sponge for bailing, and a repair kit consisting of extra bark, gum, and *watap* (spruce root used for sewing the seams). Then there is the baggage; each crewman is allowed forty pounds of it, and gentlemen get more. When they first set out, the canoes were also weighed down with more than nine hundred pounds of food, but it is mostly gone now. All of this cargo rests on long poles laid in the bottom of the craft, which bear the weight and maintain the canoe's stiffness. According to one Nor' Wester, "An European on seeing one of these slender vessels thus laden, heaped up, and sunk with her gunwale within six inches of the water, would think his fate inevitable in such a boat . . . but the Canadians are so expert that few accidents happen."[17]

To find out what is in those pieces, we need to follow the line of men shouldering the cargo up to the gate. First, stop and look at the depot—it is an impressive sight. This is "the Head-Quarters or General Rendezvous for all who commerce in this part of the World." George Nelson, an opposition clerk who visited in 1802, wrote that "the establishment of the N. W. Co., tho' there was nothing superfluous or unnecessary, . . . was of an extent to prove at once the great trade they carried on, their judgement & taste in the regularity & position of their numerous buildings. The neatness & order of things was not [the] least part of it."[18]

The first thing you see is the palisade built of fifteen-foot-long cedar logs, only twenty paces from the shore. The logs are pointed—not to spear intruders, but to shed water. There are three gates that are barred and locked after sunset. Two of them have guardhouses where sentries stand watch all night, "cheifly [*sic*] for fear of accident by fire."[19]

It all gives the place a misleadingly military air. No one ever expects this post to be attacked—particularly not by Indians, who are welcome inside as valued customers. The palisades are there to control traffic, protecting the company's inventory from pilferers, opposition spies, and any riotous behavior from the company's own men. They also separate the classes. Inside, the dominant language changes from French to English, and you suddenly see men dressed in knee pants, stockings and buckled shoes, long-tailed coats with shiny brass buttons, cravats, and hats.

The depot is a crowded, bustling village. The best description of it was written by a clerk named John Macdonell in 1793: "The buildings within the Fort are sixteen in number made with cedar and white spruce fir split with whip saws after being squared, the Roofs are couvered with shingles of Cedar and Pine, most of their posts, Doors, and windows, are painted with spanish brown. Six of these buildings are Store Houses for the company's Merchandize and Furs &c. The rest are dwelling houses shops

The roof of the Great Hall rises above the palisades marking the perimeter of the reconstructed fur trade depot.

Looking toward the lake along the eastern palisade wall

compting house and Mess House." Another visitor added that the "Dwelling Houses, Shops & Stores &c. all . . . appear to be temporary buildings, just to serve for this moment."[20]

Here, there is shelter from the wind. From the clang of hammer on anvil you can tell that the blacksmith is busy repairing some guns, traps, or other iron tools. There is a cooperage, too, with barrel staves and hoops stacked in front. Two Indian women are sitting under an awning, watching the hubbub and talking softly in Ojibway. We will follow the moccasined feet of the voyageurs along the dusty path to the warehouse.[21]

Inside is a scene of controlled confusion. As the pieces come in, each is weighed to make sure nothing is missing. (The weights were marked on them before they left Montreal.) Some are promptly unpacked by a crew of clerks busy sorting merchandise and making up outfits for the various posts. Each *bourgeois* or department head has put in an order for next winter's trade in his district, and the clerks must assemble the goods and make sure he is accurately charged. Some trusted men are making up new bales for the clerks to mark with the company's name, the year, the district they're bound to, and their weight. As yet there are few furs here; they are being stored at the other end of the portage. As these warehouses empty of goods they will gradually fill with furs. The packages for the farthest posts have to go off first. The onset of winter is an unforgiving deadline, and it comes as early as October in some parts of the country.[22]

Step closer to see what they are packing. One *bourgeois'* shopping list from 1801 called for "coarse woollen cloths of different kinds; milled blankets of different sizes; arms and ammunition; twist and carrot tobacco; Man-

A picket from the original palisade wall excavated in 1936

Tools of the clerk's trade: (from top) a candlestick base and candle snuffer, found at the site of Fort Charlotte, and an inkwell, excavated at Grand Portage, that was designed for use with a quill pen.

chester goods [cotton]; linens, and coarse sheetings; thread, lines and twine; common hardware; cutlery and ironmongery of several descriptions; kettles of brass and copper, and sheet-iron; silk and cotton handkerchiefs; hats, shoes and hose; calicoes and printed cottons, &c. &c. &c." And, of course, "Spirituous liquors."[23]

It is worth noting that six out of fourteen categories in this list are cloth. Proud as the traders are of their flintlock guns, the truth is they mainly run blanket and fabric shops. The other thing to note is that this list omits mention of goods most traders think of as "women's"—beads, needles, awls, ribbons, jewelry, vermilion. These are among the most profitable items carried.[24]

Leaving, we'll pass other warehouses: one holds enough liquor to float the company's ship, another is piled with food to provision the northern brigades. Gunpowder is kept in a powder house well away from any fires. In the off-season, account books are stored there for safekeeping.[25]

We have already met some clerks. They are the lowest members of the fur trade's upper class. Many are young, for it is an entry-level position. They all lodge together in a dormitory-like building within the stockade. Some of them are "sober decent young Gentlemen." Others, for the first time "freed from the shackels of a Strict parent," are beginning to "run riot" and indulge in "all the foolish & vulgar language of the lowest of our crew." Still others are homesick teenagers who are constantly "chasing back a flood of tears." It is an uncertain time for them. Though they're hard at work, they don't yet know where or with whom they will be spending the winter.[26]

There are more clerks at work as we enter the countinghouse. It is an office lined with tall writing stands holding huge, leather-bound ledgers. The floor is gritty with blotting sand, and the clerks' fingers are black with ink. Here is where all the accounting is done. This is a complex job, for each district has separate accounts, and the furs coming in belong to a different year's accounts than the goods going out. The job is made even more complex by the variety of currencies in use. The lower classes are paid in French currency—francs, livres, louis, and sous—while the gentlemen use British—pounds, shillings, and pence. But Spanish dollars or piasters are also used, and the British currency is divided into two valuations, Halifax and sterling. Then, because of the inflated prices in the west, a new kind of currency has come into use there: Grand Portage Currency, or G.P.C. Twelve pounds G.P.C. equals one pound sterling. One hundred pounds G.P.C. can buy a colt, and six hundred to one thousand is a typical yearly wage for an *engagé*.[27]

The countinghouse is also the equivalent of a personnel department. Here is where all the winterers must come to settle their accounts. If they

have bought anything from the company over the winter the price is de-
ducted from their wages, and if anything is left over they can either get *bons*
to spend here or drafts to send home. They can also sign new contracts. All
supervisors are supposed to have their men's accounts straight before
coming down to Grand Portage, but they often don't do it and have to be
nagged.[28]

There is one class of person we have not yet met: the *bourgeois* or partners, the elite of Grand Portage society. They are the owners of the company,
both the shareholders and management. They are about to hold a meeting
in the Great Hall, so we will peek in on them.[29]

It sounds as if we have stumbled upon a suburb of Inverness: the Scottish accents are thick enough to cut. All are talking at a great rate. For one
thing, most of them have been isolated for months, directing their departments in the west, and this is their one chance to socialize. But it is
also serious business. The exchange of information is almost as important
at Grand Portage as the exchange of goods. They're talking about which re-
gions had the best returns last winter, who had conflicts with the Indians,
where food was scarce, what sorts of goods sold best, how the opposition
did. Every year the company's distribution of posts and goods changes in
response to changing conditions. If the company is not well coordinated,
two posts can end up competing while another region is left without
traders.[30]

They're also gossiping hard about each other. At their annual meeting
important personnel changes will be made. Some partners will retire, others will go on leave according to a strict rotation system. They will have to
decide which clerks to promote or whether to reward a successful partner with another share in the company. There is a lot of lobbying. One fac-
tion suspects another of intending to promote a partisan clerk despite his
obvious incompetence, and they're collecting votes to block the move.
Some partners are campaigning to get certain districts. The factions often
break down along family lines, for a good many of these men are related.[31]

There is a stir as a new person enters: the agent from Montreal we saw
arriving. The men in the room greet him as "Mr. McGillivray." He is a
representative of the firm of McTavish, Frobisher and Company, the North
West Company's Montreal supplier. McTavish, Frobisher now has two
agents here; the other one, Mr. Mackenzie, has been supervising depot operations since early June. These two are the North West Company's link to
the east. They are also the most powerful men here, since their firm holds
almost half the shares in the North West Company. The talk now shifts, for
Mr. McGillivray has news about how furs are selling in London and
Moscow and how tariffs, insurance, and government regulations are af-
fecting the trade. He is also gathering information. The wintering part-

Ojibway dancers during
Rendezvous Days at
Grand Portage National
Monument in the 1970s

ners' news about the quantities and kinds of goods the Indians are buying influences the overseas orders his company will place this fall. The Indians are exacting customers, and their needs and tastes are unlike those of Europeans. Whenever war or disease breaks out among the Indians, it has a ripple effect in London, Lisbon, and Holland.[32]

The sound of drums from outside interrupts the talk. An Ojibway delegation has gathered in the open square before the Great Hall to perform an honor dance for the visiting dignitaries. The men's clothes are bright with feathers, quillwork, and beads, and they jingle with tiny hawk bells as they move. The women wear cloth dresses fringed with metal cones cut from kettles, which make a swishing, tinkling sound. As the drums start to beat, a crowd forms. The gentlemen come out to stand on the porch of the Great Hall and watch. At the end, they present the dancers with a ceremonial gift of shrub (rum punch) and invite the chief inside. There they will exchange elaborate speeches and gifts. The chief will present them with furs

The Grand Portage trail in the summertime

and they will present him with a uniform coat, a hat, and other marks of distinction.[33]

We will leave them talking and head on. As we pass by the kitchen complex, the smell of baking bread is mouthwatering. You also catch a whiff of fresh-cut hay and manure from the barn. The company doesn't do a lot of farming here; the men say that "nothing but potatoes have been found to answer the trouble of cultivation." They do have livestock, though: horses and oxen for hauling loads, sheep and pigs for meat, and cows for milk, butter, and beef. The animals numbered twenty-three in 1787, and probably there are more by now.[34]

As we come near the north gate, we have to sidestep a moving line of men almost buried under huge packs. They are setting off on the portage, so we follow. It is hard work keeping up. They move at a fast trot through the northmen's camp, across the stream, and into the woods.

The ninety-pound pieces are balanced high on each man's back, the lowest one being tied to a strong leather strap called a tumpline or portage collar, which passes across the man's forehead. (The idea was borrowed from Indian women, who traditionally carried a family's belongings from camp to camp.) The men walk bent forward with knees flexed, balancing most of the weight on their shoulders. "He is not looked upon as 'a man' who cannot carry two [pieces]," wrote one trader. "There are many who even take three and outrun their fellows." When the men get to competing with each other, they can travel the Grand Portage and return, fully loaded, "in the course of six hours, being a distance of eighteen miles over hills and mountains."[35]

Under normal circumstances, the trip is more leisurely. The men stop about every half hour at a place on the trail called a pose; the Grand Portage has sixteen of them. As we catch up with the pork eaters at the first pose, we find them smoking their pipes and doing a certain amount of grousing. As one traveler noted, "The young men . . . now began to regret that they had enlisted into this service, which requires them, as they say, to carry burdens like horses, when, by remaining in their own country, they might have laboured like men."[36]

The company did try to use wagons or oxcarts on this trail but "without success." Horses and oxen were "only useful for light, bulky articles; or for transporting upon sledges, during the winter, whatever goods may remain there." In later years, there are a few mentions of a "public Road" fit for carts and wagons, but little is known about it.[37]

The first part of the trail runs almost due north, following the creek, but soon it angles off to the west. There are landmarks along the way: the parting trees, the fountain, the meadow. The first written description of the trail, in 1775, said that it "consists in two ridges of land, between which is a deep glen or valley, with good meadowlands, and a broad stream of water. The lowlands are covered chiefly with birch and poplar, and the high with pine." Others found it a less sylvan scene, especially as its intensive use increased. In 1800 "the Portage was very bad in some places, knee deep in mud and clay, and so slippery, as to make walking tedious." Another traveler complained that "where it is not rock, it is mud." The mosquitoes are "ferocious."[38]

The time it takes to carry over the goods for each district's brigade varies: "seven days of severe and dangerous exertion" for one group, "five day's hard labor" for another. In 1784 the North West Company could get the baggage for all its brigades across in fifteen days, but those times are long gone.[39]

The sight of the Pigeon River through the trees is a welcome one. The trail comes down the north bank of Snow Creek, passes the North West Company's Fort Charlotte, and meets the river at a large wooden dock. The fort, named for the wife of George III, must remain a mystery until archaeological research reveals its nature. Almost no written record of it survives. The most detailed description (by traveler George Heriot, who did not stop here) says only that it is "a stockaded quadrangle, with buildings and stores within it." Another source adds that there are "extensive Stores for Furs & Goods." We know it must have warehouses, a yard for storing and repairing canoes, and living quarters. From time to time opposition companies also put up posts across the creek.[40]

The dock area is a scene of bustle and confusion, for a brigade is about to set out. On the grass some men are working on their upended canoes, patching holes with birch bark and *watap,* then caulking the seams with a mixture of pine pitch, tallow, and charcoal heated on a fire. Other canoes are pulled up at the dock for loading. These are the North canoes used throughout the west—smaller than Montreal canoes, but still bigger than modern ones. They are twenty-five feet long and are paddled by four to six men. They can carry about 3,700 pounds but are light enough for two men to haul over a portage. As you peer in, you can see that the twenty-three to twenty-five pieces of goods they carry is only two-thirds of the load. The rest is food and baggage.[41]

Each brigade is made up of four to eight canoes, and their departure is carefully spaced two days apart to prevent the portages inland from getting crowded. When two groups use the same portage at once, pieces inevitably get mixed up or left behind. The brigades bound for the farthest posts set off first. On the first day they only go as far as a spot called "the Prairie," just beyond Partridge Falls, where they make "merry upon some small Kegs of Wines which is generally given them on their engagement at G[rand] P[ortage], and one and sometimes 2 Gallons to each man." This "regale" is "generally enjoyed at this spot where we have a delightful Meadow to pitch our Tents and plenty of elbow room for the men to play their antic tricks."[42]

No sooner has the brigade set out than we see another group of canoes coming downstream, loaded with furs. With a good deal of exuberant swearing the men pull up at the dock and begin to unload. Their furs have all been pressed into bales. Though the pelts were cleaned by Indian women to prevent them from rotting, the smell is strong. There are things besides furs, too: kegs of castoreum, a liquid from the glands of beavers, used in perfume making and for baiting traps, and some bags of pemmican and buffalo grease for provisioning outgoing brigades. The furs will be stored here at Fort Charlotte till the pork eaters shuttle them back across the portage. At the other end they will all be sorted and inventoried, checked against the *bourgeois'* accounts, then remade into bales for shipment to Montreal, where they will arrive in September.[43]

We will follow the northmen who are heading across the portage, carrying only their own baggage and looking forward to being "regaled with plenty, and feasted on bread and pork . . . and a *coup* to make them merry." By the time we reach the main depot again, the dinner bell is ringing and people are flocking toward the Great Hall. We have to leave our *engagé*

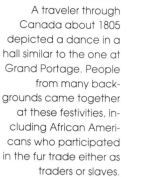

A traveler through Canada about 1805 depicted a dance in a hall similar to the one at Grand Portage. People from many backgrounds came together at these festivities, including African Americans who participated in the fur trade either as traders or slaves.

companions behind, for only the higher ranks are allowed to eat in the Great Hall.[44]

The long room is crowded with tables. Almost a hundred well-dressed men are standing by their chairs in a hush of expectation, their eyes on the head table. At last the *bourgeois* enter, dressed "fit to appear at court," and take their seats. With a thunderous scraping of chair legs on the board floors, the rest then sit down. Everyone is arranged strictly by rank: *bourgeois* at one table, head clerks next, then apprentice clerks, interpreters, and guides. Their manners are formal; they are careful to refer to everyone above them in the social scale as "Mister." The North West Company's "strict rules of subordination" are never forgotten.[45]

The white tablecloths are set with pewter utensils, pearlware dishes from England, Chinese porcelain, and stemmed wine glasses. The menu consists of "bread, salt pork, beef, hams, fish, and venison, butter, peas, Indian corn, potatoes, tea, spirits, wine, &c. and plenty of milk." As one clerk put it, "the best of every thing and the best of fish." There is plenty of imported Spanish and Canary wine, too.[46]

On most nights, when dinner is over the tablecloths are removed and the lower ranks leave. Then the *bourgeois,* along with some select head clerks, will start drinking in earnest, while the other clerks relax outside, "cracking their jokes at the expense of their superiors." There's a lot of after-

An Ojibway camp in the 1840s included dwellings covered with birch bark; the tent on the right was probably that of the artist, Paul Kane.

dinner talk; most of the men are old friends, and as one said, "when People meet in this Country as it is so seldom not a moment is to be lost, but improved by keeping up an agreeable (if possible) conversation, and in smoking the sociable Pipe." Their talks give them "much the same satisfaction and delight that two old Soldiers have when they meet after a long separation."[47]

But when dinner is over tonight, everyone leaves and the servants start clearing away tables and lighting lamps for a North West ball. "This evening the Gentlemen of the place dressed & we had a famous Ball in the Dining Room," wrote one clerk. "For musick we had the Bag-Pipe the Violin, the Flute & the Fife, which enabled us to spend the evening agreeably." Dancing is the main attraction: jigs, reels, and hornpipes set to rollicking Celtic tunes, danced stiff-armed and with fancy footwork. The men's partners are "this Countries *Ladies*"—the Indian and mixed-blood wives and daughters of traders. They are polite, doubtless stylishly dressed, and "danced not amiss." Now and then the bagpipe will break off and play a mournful Scottish ballad, and everyone will sing. Liquor is never absent; soon all are thoroughly mellow.[48]

Outside, the light from the windows lies golden on the porch. Out on the bay the moon is painting a path of silver across the lake. Climbing up into the guardhouse where the fire watch is on duty, we can see campfires dotting the beach like stars. The strains of an old French *chanson* rise from one of the camps, competing with the muffled fiddle music from the Great Hall. There is a sound of drumming from one cluster of campfires, and we realize there is still one place to visit. The guard will let us out the gate so we can walk through the cricket-filled darkness to the Ojibway camp.

As we approach, some dogs run up to greet us. We thread our way past drying racks, where the women were smoking fish today. Some of the houses are tipi-shaped but covered with huge sheets of birch bark instead of skin. Others are long A-frame structures covered with bark and woven rush mats. These are big enough to house several related families at once. The largest is a "Grand Lodge," where feasts and public ceremonies are held.[49]

A lot of the people are outside. One crowd is gathered around a campfire where four men are playing the moccasin game. While one man hides a marked bullet under one of four moccasins, his partner drums and sings in a high falsetto voice. As the music reaches a crescendo, their opponent strikes one of the moccasins with a stick, guessing that is where the special bullet is hidden. They keep score with marked sticks. Everyone is wagering heavily on the teams. The onlookers are all dressed in cloth, but the effect is not European. The women wear calf-length dresses held up by shoulder straps and decorated with intricate ribbon appliqué. The men wear calico shirts, woolen loincloths, and beaded bags. If it were colder, the women would put on detachable sleeves and the men would wear leggings. The firelight glints on their silver jewelry and beads.

In the shadows behind one lodge a teenaged boy and girl are whispering to each other, heads close. Another boy is softly playing a courting flute outside the house of a girl he fancies. The evidence of the day's work is all around: fishnets hanging out to dry, copper pails of berries sitting high on food racks, a half-finished canoe staked out on the ground, a moose-skin stretched on a drying rack. Despite this, there is an air of leisure, of time to spare, that contrasts with the harried bustle of the post.

We lift the blanket hung at the door of one house, and the residents welcome us hospitably. The interior is lit by two campfires, and on the floor are fresh cedar boughs that give off a pungent scent at every step. The woman of the house offers us some wooden bowls of fish soup, then settles back to some handwork she is making to sell at the post; the gentlemen like to take Indian souvenirs when they go back east. The women's conversation, spoken in Ojibway and Cree, is mostly about the Indian families who are constantly coming and going. In the rear of the lodge some men trade stories about the animals they killed last winter, the ones that got away, and adventures with frostbite and forest. One old man pipes up with the story of how he once killed a bear with only a knife. They've all heard it before but listen politely.[50]

This is why the fur trade exists: these are the people who buy the goods, make the canoes, hunt the animals, and cure the skins. They guide the traders along the waterways and supply them with food through the winter. The depot and all the people in it collect and transport the products of Indian labor. The white people make a lot more bustle and noise, but the fur trade is really an Indian industry. If the Indian life-style should cease to exist, so would the fur trade.

It is late, time to leave our hosts and their century behind. The intricate mesh of jobs, languages, and people that is the fur trade has only about fifty more years to exist in this region. But before we return to our own time, perhaps we should look even farther back to find out how this vast cooperative commerce first came about.

# CHAPTER TWO

# First Contact

If histories of North America were written fairly, they would begin not with the nations of Europe but the nations of this land. In 1640 the Great Lakes region was a complex patchwork of territories belonging to powerful, populous confederacies: Iroquois, Algonquian, Huron, Ottawa, Dakota. It was they who shaped the fur trade.

North of the lakes dwelt the many allied groups who spoke Algonquian languages—among them the Cree, Ottawa, Ojibway, Menominee, Potawatomie, and Nipissing. They were hunters, fishermen, and traders, inventors of the birch-bark canoe and experts of the waterways. South of the lakes lived semiagricultural village dwellers—the Dakota, Fox, Winnebago, Miami, and the tribes of the powerful Iroquois league. Neither fences nor maps delineated the boundaries between these groups, but the lines were no less real for being immaterial. There was no love lost between the Algonquians and their southern neighbors. The Algonquian word for Iroquois was *Nadoweg,* or adder; the word for Dakota was *Nadouessioux,* or like an Iroquois.[1]

In the earliest written records Lake Superior is called *Lac des Nadouessioux* for the Dakota people who occupied its southern and western shores. On the north shore lived the Cree. West of the lake, the border line between these groups ran approximately along the present international boundary. In the seventeenth century Rainy Lake was called *Lac des Cristinaux* for the Cree, and Lake of the Woods was *Lac des Assiniboiles,* for the Assiniboine, a group of Yanktonai Dakota who had splintered off and become allies of the Cree, enemies of their old kinsmen.[2] Grand Portage, lying in the contested zone between the Cree and Dakota, was thus at a strategic location. It and the Kaministikwia River were the only routes the Assiniboine and other, more western tribes could take to the Great Lakes.

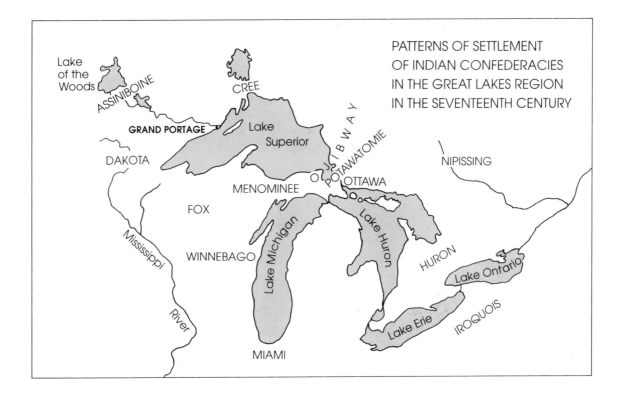

PATTERNS OF SETTLEMENT OF INDIAN CONFEDERACIES IN THE GREAT LAKES REGION IN THE SEVENTEENTH CENTURY

Despite political tensions, commerce flourished among the communities. The southerly tribes traded corn and tobacco for dried meat and skins. Northerners could always sell crafted articles like fishnets, snowshoes, and birch-bark containers. The Ottawa and Huron traded with the Winnebago of Wisconsin for "light earthen pots, and girdles made of goat's hairs, and small shells that grow att the sea side." The Ojibway and Cree were sought out for medicines.[3]

Trade was an old activity in North America. Over the years economic strategies, trading routes, and customs had become entrenched. When the French arrived on the St. Lawrence River, eager to barter their blankets, nightcaps, sheets, swords, axes, kettles, prunes, and crackers for Indian furs, they could do nothing but adapt. They could not have imposed a European-style trading system on the Great Lakes if they had tried. The Huron and Algonquians became their mentors, middlemen, and protectors.[4]

## Binding Ties

Present-day entrepreneurs would find the trading system that the French encountered very alien. To begin with, many sales strategies that we now take for granted didn't work.

If European-style merchants want to sell more, they cut prices. If they want their suppliers to produce more, they pay more. If goods are scarce, prices are expected to rise; if they are plentiful, prices will go down. None of these axioms of economics worked in North America, for a simple reason: all are based on the assumption that the customer's desire for goods is limited only by his or her ability to pay. But Indian customers did not want to accumulate unlimited material goods.

This choice was partly due to their life-style. When a family moves six or seven times a year, possessions are merely more inconvenient baggage. But much more important were cultural values. In Indian society, property ownership was not the route to power or prestige. Community leaders were expected to share all they had. Gift giving was applauded, hoarding was condemned. Children were not promised material rewards. Praise and honor were the motivating forces, and these were refined into as many gradations and symbolic expressions as we have material status symbols today. Shame was far worse than poverty.[5]

Huron women traveling with their children and possessions on their backs. The tumpline or leather strap across the forehead was adopted by voyageurs as a way to balance heavy loads on their shoulders.

The result could be ruinous to European traders. When costs went up and a trader raised prices, the Indians often saw it as an act of bad faith and refused to buy. When prices went down, they did not stock up but merely bought as much as they needed for the present. "People would suppose it would rouse their attention to industry, having goods at a lower price, but far to the contrary," wrote one disgruntled trader. Others accused the Indians of "laziness" and "improvidence"—the angry businessman's code words for "nonmaterialistic." The Indians' refusal to become embroiled in the European economic system was to frustrate traders for two hundred years.[6]

But the failure of the usual European sales techniques didn't mean there was no way to stimulate trade. The traders merely had to find what motivated their customers. The answer lay in another characteristic of commerce. Nowhere is it an entirely secular, politically meaningless, morally neutral activity. It is always entwined with sociopolitical values.

In Indian society, trade was a public ceremony. To open trade was to cement an alliance—a relationship imbued with many mutual obligations, including political and military aid, social duties such as food sharing, and intermarriage. Politics and trade were inseparable, as the French soon found out when they became entangled along with their Algonquian partners in a war against the Iroquois.

They also found themselves enmeshed in a fabric of kinship. In native American society, family was a civil body as well as a biological one. It was, in fact, the Indian equivalent of a legal and judicial system. The family enforced codes of behavior. If you were injured, it was your family's obligation to seek either revenge or reparation. If you injured another person your entire family was jeopardized, since the victim could legitimately punish any of your kin. You were expected to treat kin in a moral, altruistic fashion, sharing food and taking their part in disputes. Where no kinship ties existed, you could act in a self-interested, exploitative way.[7]

It was to both the traders' and the Indians' advantage to be considered each other's kin. To the trader, the relationship meant the difference between being outside and inside the law. To the Indian, it meant a trader was obligated to support his extended family in need. It was easier for a European to join an Indian family than vice versa. Marriage was one route into the system. Another was adoption, an institution so respected that, according to an Ojibway writer, "Whenever these ties have been disregarded or grossly violated, the occurrence is told in their lodge tales, in terms to teach the rising generation never to do likewise." Though European society had no similar entrée for Indians, native people tried to incorporate themselves into an imaginary French "family" by addressing Canada's governor as "Father" and referring to themselves as his children. Unfortunately, this rhetoric seldom excited the intended sense of parental obligation.[8]

During the 1600s most trading occurred at French towns along the St. Lawrence, particularly Montreal and Quebec. Large tribal delegations traveled east to meet the French governor and bargain directly with merchants. The customs followed in these visits set the tone for the fur trade to come.

Trade was a highly stylized activity. Once, when the French tried to hurry the process, the Huron "expostulated against the methods of our merchants in completing the trade in an hour." The elaborate etiquette often included a feast, the smoking of pipes, and the exchange of generous gifts. All were highly symbolic. The sharing of food cemented kinship and political ties; as one astute trader observed, "without the help of the pot you cannot have friendship." The pipe solemnized the occasion, calling on sacred powers to witness. The gifts reflected honor upon the giver and created respect for his position, but they were also invitations to reciprocity. Gifts remained a crucial part of the Indian-white relationship.[9]

Then the oratory started. The French found Indian trade rhetoric startling. The Indians' first strategy was usually to shame the traders into generosity, using a concept in Indian ethics called (in the Ojibway language) *jawendjige,* to take pity. Nicolas Perrot, who spent more than thirty years trading with the Great Lakes tribes, described its use between two Indian groups. The Dakota, who were trying to open trade with the Ottawa, "began, according to their custom, to weep over every person they met, in order to manifest the lively joy which they felt in meeting them; and they entreated the strangers to have pity on them." When the Ottawa gave the Dakota gifts, the latter "declared that they placed great value on these, lifting their eyes to the sky, and blessing it for having guided to their country these peoples." The Dakota "loaded them with endearing terms, and showed the utmost submissiveness, in order to touch them with compassion and obtain from them some benefits."[10]

Unaccustomed to such behavior, traders at first tended to take it all at face value. When an Indian delegation wept and said families were starving, the traders believed it. When the Indians called them gods, they half believed that, too. Many mistook the rhetoric for subordination or begging. They were wrong—it was partly polite manipulation and partly insistence that the traders live up to the social obligations they had incurred by opening the trade relationship. If it didn't work, the Indians turned to other strategies. They invoked past favors and played rival traders off against one another. As early as 1611 the French were complaining that "these Indians are now too sharp and crafty" in their bargaining.[11]

The French had their own trade rhetoric. In contrast to the Indians', it consisted of extolling themselves and their goods. "Throw aside your bone bodkins," Nicolas Perrot told some Mascouten women. "These French

Goods that French traders commonly traded to the Indians in exchange for furs, as reported in 1703 by the adventurer Louis-Armand de Lom d'Arce, baron de Lahontan. "Fusee" was the English term for *fusil*, or musket.

[258] Short and light Fufees.
Powder.
Ball and cut Lead, or Small-fhot.
Axes both great and fmall.
Knives with their Sheaths.
Sword-blades to make Darts of.
Kettles of all fizes.
Shoomakers Awls.
Fifh-hooks, of all fizes.
Flint Stones.
Caps of blew Serge.
Shirts made of the common *Brittany* Linnen.
Woolfted Stockins, fhort and coarfe.
*Brafil* Tobacco.
Coarfe white Thread for Nets.
Sewing Thread of feveral colours.
Pack-thread.
Vermillion.
Needles, both large and fmall.
*Venice* Beads.
Some Iron Heads for Arrows, but few of 'em.
A fmall quantity of Soap.
A few Sabres or Cutlaffes.
   Brandy goes off incomparably well.

awls will be much easier to use. . . . To you who are old men I leave my kettle; I carry it everywhere without fear of breaking it." Perrot swept grandly from tribe to tribe, spreading a gospel in which trade was redemption: "The sun has never been very bright on your horizon; you have always been

---

THE Skins of Winter Beavers, *alias Muscovy* Beavers, are worth *per pound* in the Farmer Generals Warehouse. — — — — 4 *Livres.* 10 *Sous.*

| | | |
|---|---|---|
| The Skins of fat Beavers, the Hair of which falls off, while the Savages make use of 'em, *per pound*,[1] | 5 *L.* | 0 *S.* |
| Of Beavers taken in Autumn, *per pound* — — | 3 | 10 |
| [259] Of dry or common Beavers, *per pound* — | 3 | 0 |
| Of Summer Beavers, *per pound.* — — — | 3 | 0 |

The Skin of a white Beaver is not to be valued, no more than that of a Fox that's quite black.

| | | |
|---|---|---|
| The Skins of Silver-colour'd Foxes a piece. — | 4 | 0 |
| Of common Foxes, in good order, — — — | 2 | 0 |
| Of the common Martins. — — — — | 1 | 0 |
| Of the prettyeft fort of Martins. — — — | 4 | 0 |
| Of red and fmooth Otters. — — — — | 2 | 0 |
| Of the Winter and brown Otters. — — — or more. | 4 | 10 |
| Of the fineft black Bears. — — — — | 7 | 0 |
| The Skins of Elks before they're drefs'd, are worth *per pound* about. — — — — — | 0 | 12 |
| The Skins of Stags are worth *per pound* about — | 0 | 8 |
| The wild Cats or *Enfans de Diable*, a piece — | 1 | 15 |
| Sea Wolves — a piece. — — — — or more. | 1 | 15 |
| Pole-Cats, and Weafels — — — — | 0 | 10 |
| Musk Rats. — — — — — — | 0 | 6 |
| Their Tefticles. — — — — — | 0 | 5 |
| Wolves. — — — — — — | 2 | 10 |
| The white Elk-skins, *i. e.* thofe drefs'd by the Savages a piece — — — — — — | 8 or m. | |
| A drefs'd Harts Skin is worth — — — | 5 or m. | |
| A Caribous — — — — — | 6 | |
| A Roe-buck's — — — — — — | 3 | |

To conclude, you muft take notice that thefe Skins are upon fome particular occafions dearer than I rate 'em, but the difference is but very fmall, whether under or over.[1]

---

Lahontan's account of the value of different kinds of furs

wrapped in the shadows of a dark and miserable existence, never having enjoyed the true light of day, as the French do. . . . I am the dawn of that light, which is beginning to appear in your lands . . . who will soon shine brightly and will cause you to be born again, as if in another land, where you will find, more easily and in greater abundance, all that can be necessary to man."[12]

Extravagant as Perrot's rhetoric was, he probably believed a good portion of it. The French, and other Europeans who followed them, were unshakably convinced of the superiority of their own technology. The sight of Fox women slicing meat with their exquisitely sharp flint knives struck Perrot as pitiful. The Indians did not see it that way. They valued trade goods, as one Frenchman observed, "not so much for their novelty as for the convenience they derived therefrom." Convenience is the key word. The goods did not radically alter Indian ways of life but made those ways more convenient. There is little plausible evidence that Indians depended on these items or starved without them, as self-important traders sometimes claimed. A century later traders were still struggling to keep their customers from going back to older technologies. Traders had to live in Indian villages, a British merchant argued, in order to "excite a desire in them to have the commodities of Europe . . . without which they would . . . only hunt for sustenance and a few skins to make themselves cloathing."[13]

In 1671 Perrot acted as translator for the French at a grand convocation of the Lake Superior tribes, held at Sault Ste. Marie. It was the opening of formal diplomatic relations with the Cree, Monsoni, Nipissing, Ojibway, and other northwestern tribes. The Indians believed the French were asking "for permission to trade in the country, and for free passage to and from their villages." The French believed they were taking possession of the land in the name of Louis XIV. Ojibway oral tradition preserved Perrot's words in recognizable form until the speech was written down in the 1850s. The Ojibway cited it as evidence of how well the French had "assimilated themselves to the customs and mode of life" of the Indians.[14]

But it was only rhetoric.

## The Ojibway Empire

By the time the French arrived in the Lake Superior country, the fur trade was already thriving there. From the beginning, the French depended upon Indian middlemen to bring them furs from the west. During the first half of the seventeenth century the Huron had organized convoys to carry furs to Montreal. But a ruinous war with the Iroquois scattered the Huron in 1648–49, and another league took over the middleman position. Their very name, Ottawa, meant trader.[15]

The middlemen played a crucial—and profitable—role. They were not hunters but shippers and brokers, accustomed to bargaining with both Indians and Europeans. Typically, middlemen tried to keep their position by preventing direct contact between the French and client tribes. The Huron had done so by spreading rumors that the French were "unsociable, rude, sad, melancholy people who lived only on serpents and poison." The Ottawa strategy was to open up new markets far west of where the French had set foot.[16]

The French were aware of their dependence on the Ottawa, who "alone supply us with two-thirds of the Beaver that is sent to France." "They get their peltries, in the North, from the people of the interior," one official reported, adding that "they go in search of it to the most distant places."[17]

One of those "distant places" was, very likely, Grand Portage. In the 1660s one group of Ottawa set up headquarters at Chequamegon Bay on the south shore of Lake Superior. From there, the middlemen made trading expeditions north and west. They visited Lake Nipigon, where, according to Perrot's rather owlish report, they secured from the residents "all their beaver robes for old knives, blunted awls, wretched nets, and kettles used until they were past service. For these they were most humbly thanked." They probably rendezvoused with the Cree and Assiniboine at Grand Portage.[18]

But the Ottawa's domination, like that of the Huron, was undermined by war—this time with the Dakota and Fox. In 1671 the Ottawa abandoned their insecure outpost on Lake Superior, opening up the way for a new and more lasting middleman empire. This time it was the Ojibway.

A Paris furrier's shop in the mid-1700s as depicted in an engraving in Denis Diderot's *Encyclopédie*. Boxes holding muffs line the walls.

The French first met the ancestors of the Ojibway along the north shore of Lake Huron and at the strategic junction of Lakes Michigan, Huron, and Superior. They did not call themselves Ojibway, but went by the names of their many small, independent villages organized around clan groups, including the Awause (Catfish), Amik (Beaver), and Noka (Bear). These clan-villages eventually gave rise to the Ottawa and Potawatomie tribes as well as the Ojibway. (In those early times the tribal divisions of today had not yet solidified.) In all three tribes, many of the ancient clans still survive.[19]

By the 1660s the proto-Ojibway had begun to consolidate at Sault Ste. Marie, where the fisheries supported a summer population of one thousand or more. When the French established a mission there, they called the people *Saulteurs* (people of the falls). The Ojibway called the French *Wametigoshe* (people of the waving stick, for the priests' crosses).[20]

In the 1670s this small, obscure tribe began a westward expansion that would continue until the group occupied an area from Ontario to Montana, the largest geographical distribution of any tribe in North America. Their energetic participation in the fur trade was one motive for this expansion.[21]

The tribe divided at the Sault, part going along the North Shore of Lake Superior, part along the south. They were not to meet again for about sixty years—three generations—when they both reached Grand Portage. By then the two groups, who may have stemmed from different clan villages to begin with, had contrasting life-styles and dialects. The north-shore Ojibway depended entirely on hunting, fishing, and gathering. They lived in small, widely scattered groups and maintained a system of family hunting territories. The south-shore Ojibway hunted and fished but also farmed, gathered wild rice, and made maple sugar. They lived in large summer villages, where they gathered yearly to celebrate the rites of their religious and curing society, the *Midéwiwin.*

The north-shore Ojibway were probably first to reach Grand Portage. In 1736 a group of the Awause clan had a summer village at the present site of Thunder Bay, where they probably traded as middlemen to the Cree. The Caribou clan, today common at Grand Portage, was said to be part of this northern group, as was the Pike clan.[22]

The south-shore Ojibway had a more eventful journey. The Dakota, who (according to crusty old Perrot) were "not very solicitous for the friendship of any one whomsoever," at first opposed their movement west. But in 1679 the Dakota met the Ojibway in a council at the present site of Duluth. There, the tribes hammered out an agreement. The Dakota would allow the Ojibway access to their hunting lands along Lake Superior. In return, the Ojibway would supply them with French trade goods.[23]

Buttressing the Ojibway position in the council was the presence of a Frenchman, Daniel Greysolon, sieur Du Lhut, a soldier turned independent trader. His friends described him as a man "of inviolable fidelity," and his enemies called him a deserter and illegal trader. After leaving the council he coasted up the north shore, passed Grand Portage, and established a trading fort at the mouth of the Kaministikwia River, where Thunder Bay now stands. Traveling up the Kaministikwia, he met with the Assiniboine and negotiated for their furs.[24]

Meanwhile, some of the Ojibway established a town on Chequamegon Bay, near the old headquarters of the Ottawa. The Ojibway commercial alliance with the Dakota lasted for fifty-seven years. During that peace they flourished, and trade flourished with them.

## The King's Estate

Du Lhut was not the first Frenchman to pass by Grand Portage. In 1660 a group of Ottawa and Huron took two young Frenchmen—Pierre Esprit, sieur de Radisson, and his brother-in-law, Médard Chouart, sieur des Groseilliers—on a lucrative but illegal (unlicensed) trading tour of Lake Superior. Whether they passed Grand Portage is uncertain, but they did meet with some northern Indians (probably Cree) who told them of an alternate route into the continent via Hudson Bay. When the pair returned to Quebec, the French government slapped them with heavy fines for unlicensed trading. Disgruntled at this treatment, Radisson took his information to England, where he found investors who persuaded Charles II to charter a new company. Starting in 1670, the Hudson's Bay Company founded a string of trading forts on the shores of Hudson and James bays, far to the north of Lake Superior.[25]

Meanwhile, back on Lake Superior, a Jesuit missionary named Claude Allouez canoed along the coast in 1667 and clearly showed the mouth of the Pigeon River on his 1670–71 map. An anonymous prospector brought back a copper sample from the Grand Portage area in 1671. In the years after Du Lhut's visit, Jacques de Noyon further developed the Kaministikwia route. In 1688 he established a post on Rainy Lake and traveled as far as Lake of the Woods.[26]

But the few who left records were far outnumbered by the shadowy *coureurs de bois*—illegal traders who were flocking west from the French settlements on the St. Lawrence. By 1680 one writer estimated there were eight hundred *coureurs* in the west. Surreptitiously supplied by Quebec merchants, these young men made two- to three-year voyages, living in Indian villages where (according to Perrot) they "made themselves like unto the savages [and] forgot what was due from them to French subordination and discipline." They made fabulous profits—figures up to 700 percent were rumored. "Where . . . there is lucre there are people enough to be had," commented Radisson. The government desperately tried to suppress them but lamented that "it is not easy to catch [them] unless we are assisted by disinterested persons; . . . the woods and the rivers afford them great facilities to escape justice."[27]

Why did the government care so much about *coureur* activity? To put it in modern terms, these men were tax evaders.

Many people have a misconception that frontiers are lawless places devoid of governmental controls. But paperwork, regulations, and tax collectors were consistently among the first things Europeans sent to their American frontiers. The French system of regulating trade was based not on modern business principles but on medieval aristocratic privilege. The St. Lawrence watershed was seen as an estate of the French king. He

A portion of the map drawn by Claude Allouez in 1670–71; "Lac Tracy" was an early name for Lake Superior.

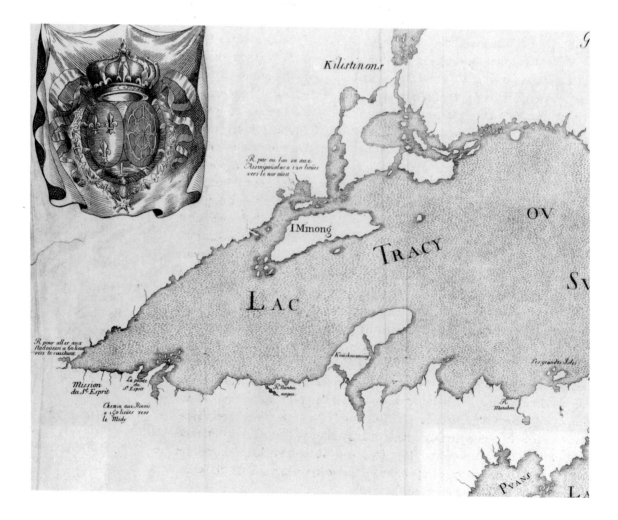

granted certain companies and individuals the right to develop its trade through a system of monopolies—a word that had a different meaning than it does today. Then, a monopoly was a license granted by the king, giving its owner the right to exclusive trade in a certain area. The monopoly holder paid the king handsomely for the privilege, hoping to recoup the expense in profits. The payment was used to finance the army and government of Canada.

The Lake Superior trade was broken up into several monopolies, each centered on a military post—Kaministikwia, Nipigon, and Chequamegon among them. Starting in the 1680s the government issued licenses, called *congés,* which allowed private merchants to send canoes west—for a price. The licenses required them to operate out of certain posts, and the furs could only be sold at fixed prices to government stores. The posts were commanded by military officers who "acted as Magistrates, compelled the Traders to deal equitably, and distributed the King's Presents" to the Indian tribes. The officers were intermediaries, "regarded by the Indians as their partner, to whom they address themselves for counsel in their affairs."[28]

But the French government constantly changed its mind about how best to regulate the fur trade. In 1696 it revoked all trading licenses and restricted trade to a few garrisoned posts in the east. In 1715 licenses were reinstated. Two years later a new commandant, Zacharie Robutel, sieur de La Noüe, came to the Kaministikwia to oversee the revival of trade. He found that while the French had been away, the Assiniboine and Cree had gotten used to trading at the English posts on Hudson Bay. There they could get higher prices for furs, cheaper goods, and better quality cloth, blankets, and kettles. The French had only one thing to offer that the English couldn't: convenience. If the Indians could "obtain their supplies at their door, they would take them, whatever the price may be." Home delivery became the French marketing strategy. And Grand Portage was to provide a means toward achieving that goal.[29]

Proposals for establishing a chain of posts from Rainy Lake to Lake Winnipeg started circulating as early as 1717. The Assiniboine and Cree, who were fighting a war with the Dakota to the south, saw trade as the route to a French military alliance. Eager to entice these Europeans to their land, they started spreading stories about the wonders of the west—mountains of sparkling stones, tribes of dwarves, and "a great river which flows straight towards the setting sun." In the late 1720s these tales fell on the receptive ears of a new commandant at Lake Nipigon—Pierre Gaultier de Varennes et de La Vérendrye. In 1729 a Cree named Auchagah gave him a map of the route connecting Lake Superior to the northwest via *Kitchi Onigaming*—the Grand Portage.[30]

## Posts of the Western Sea

The man who pioneered the fur trade route that made Grand Portage famous was not even interested in furs. La Vérendrye was, in fact, such a poor businessman that his years in the west left him deeply in debt. His real passion was geographical discovery. What he sought beyond Grand Portage was the Northwest Passage—a water route to the Orient.

"As a man he is mild and firm," wrote Charles de La Boische, marquis de Beauharnois, who, as governor of Canada, got to know La Vérendrye well. Beauharnois could have added "stubborn," as well. What the explorer didn't have was a flair for self-promotion or politics—failings that would be his downfall in the end.[31]

In 1730 La Vérendrye tried to interest the French government in financing an expedition to discover the Pacific Ocean via the "river Nantouagan"—the Cree name for the Pigeon. But Louis XV was short on cash and wanted to privatize the exploring business. Instead of money, he gave La Vérendrye a monopoly of the fur trade west of Grand Portage. The explorer would have to finance his own expedition through sale of furs. Unwarily, La Vérendrye agreed.

From the start the venture was a family affair. La Vérendrye's four sons and one nephew eventually joined him in the west. "La dame de Varennes" (presumably his wife) took care of the business in Montreal, buying licenses and organizing canoe brigades. His guide was Auchagah, "the man most capable of guiding a party" and "greatly attached to the French nation."[32]

"We arrived on the twenty-sixth of August [1731] at the Grand Portage," La Vérendrye later wrote. "All our people, in dismay at the length of the portage . . . mutinied and loudly demanded that I should turn back." This revolt delayed him several months, but by the next summer he had crossed the portage and reached Rainy Lake. From there more than fifty canoes of Cree conducted him to Lake of the Woods, where they had selected a

One version of the map drawn by Auchagah in 1729 showing the route to the northwest from Lake Superior

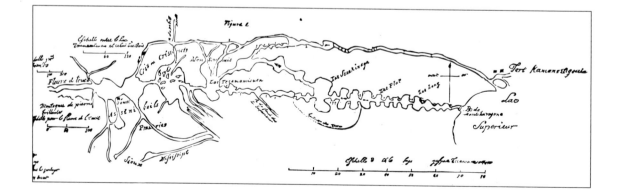

spot for him to build Fort St. Charles. He set his men to improving the waterways and portages and soon had reduced the latter from forty-one to thirty-two.[33]

The border lakes were thickly settled in those days. It wasn't unusual for three thousand people and more to gather at the posts of "La Mer de l'Ouest" that La Vérendrye established. La Marteblanche, the chief at Lake of the Woods, received him cordially, assuring him that "the Kaministik-wia road will always be a smooth one for the French" and pledging that the Cree "make one and the same body with us [the French]." To establish kinship ties they adopted Jean-Baptiste, La Vérendrye's eldest son, and petitioned the governor of Canada to reciprocate by "admit[ting] them to the number of your children."[34]

But La Vérendrye soon realized what a precarious position he was in. War parties were constantly leaving to attack the Dakota and their allies the Ojibway. The explorer preached peace but all the while did a brisk business in "powder, bullets, guns, butcher's knives, daggers, gunflints, awls, tobacco, etc." He was an arms dealer in a war zone. Nervously he wrote Quebec recommending the manning of a post on the Mississippi River, to establish good relations with the Dakota and defuse tensions. The post was established—and soon was supplying arms to the other side.[35]

In 1734 the Cree demanded that La Vérendrye live up to the implicit obligations he had undertaken by opening trade and assuming kinship with them. They asked him to send his son with them on a war party. "I was agitated, I must confess," he wrote, "and cruelly tormented by conflicting thoughts. . . . Who could tell whether my son would ever return?" And yet, if he refused, the Cree might "take the French for cowards." He finally agreed. It was a fatal mistake.[36]

In June 1736 a group of twenty-one Frenchmen led by Jean-Baptiste de La Vérendrye was attacked by a Dakota war party on an island just east of Fort St. Charles. Every one was killed. To make sure the French knew the reason, the Dakota arranged the decapitated bodies as if in a council circle and wrapped the heads in beaver skins.[37]

This was not the last time fur traders would meet with violence. But it is worth noting that it was neither random nor pointless. La Vérendrye had forfeited all claim to peaceful relations with the Dakota by dealing arms and participating in war. In almost every other instance of violence in the historical record, traders made similar mistakes.

If the French had not been integrated into the Indian system of kinship and justice, the incident of 1736 might have become just another historical footnote. But custom required their adoptive relatives and trading partners to mete out a just revenge. The result was a major realignment of political alliances on Lake Superior.

As middlemen between the French and Dakota, the Ojibway were in a delicate position. The events of 1736 forced them to choose between alliances. But it was not a very hard decision. Traders and goods had begun flowing into the Dakota country by more southerly routes. In particular, the French post on the Mississippi undercut the Ojibway middleman position. The Dakota, no longer needing them to supply trade goods, began to resent the Ojibway presence in their lands. The Ojibway, having lived there for almost three generations, were not about to leave. They decided to fight for the territory they had originally entered as guests.[38]

The Dakota-Ojibway conflict that started in 1736 was to evolve into one of the most long-lasting wars in North American history. It soon stretched along a standing front from central Wisconsin through Minnesota to the Red River of the North. By blocking all travel and trade across this line, the war had a major effect on the fur trade. It redirected traders to safer, more northerly routes—particularly the Grand Portage route. And much to the satisfaction of the Cree and Ojibway, it blocked off European access to the Dakota market.

The first group of southern Ojibway in the Grand Portage area arrived in 1736 as war refugees. They settled on the Vermilion River east of Rainy Lake. Soon they spread out to occupy the waterways from Grand Portage to Rainy Lake, with their main town at the latter spot. From there they started pushing south toward the Dakota settlements at Leech, Red, and Sandy lakes. Before forty years were up, all of northern Minnesota would be theirs.[39]

An Ojibway village stood at Grand Portage by 1742, when a French missionary wrote that the chief there was "very influential . . . a man of decision whose intrepidity produces an impression on the others." This chief planned to lead a war party gathered from bands as far away as Nipigon, Kaministikwia, and Rainy Lake. But what his name or clan was, the records do not say.[40]

The French government's reaction to the debacle on Lake of the Woods was: "most annoying." Officials quickly closed down the post among the Dakota and briefly considered recalling La Vérendrye. The only one who never seems to have considered giving up was La Vérendrye himself. After contracting with the Cree to escort canoes safely to Grand Portage each spring and fall, he turned west. The local Indians tried to stop him, assuring him that the plains tribes "did not know how to kill beaver" and "were people without intelligence." But the more westerly Cree and Assiniboine lured him on, choosing post sites, erecting buildings, and seeking out new markets for him. Before long, French forts were scattered all across western Canada at strategic points where tribal rendezvous occurred.

Ever searching for the elusive western sea, La Vérendrye sent his sons on forays up the Assiniboine and Missouri rivers. Neither seemed to be the road he sought. At last he turned to the Saskatchewan River, establishing his farthest post near present Prince Albert, Saskatchewan—a spot as far from Grand Portage as Grand Portage was from Montreal.[41]

But trouble was brewing back east. As Canada's sympathetic governor, Beauharnois, put it, "glory cannot pay the expenses." Yet the government continued to refuse financial support. Every year La Vérendrye's debts mounted. By 1739 he could barely get supplies on credit and was contending with lawsuits and warrants for the seizure of his goods to satisfy bad debts. Though he leased out the trading rights at his posts beginning in 1742, his merchant partners were often defeated by the logistical difficulties of the long distances, and La Vérendrye had to borrow money to feed his men.[42]

Worse were his political problems. The cynical French minister in Paris had no concept of the distances La Vérendrye was covering and was ready to believe the worst. He wrote that the explorer had "for several years been solely occupied with his own affairs, he has done nothing for the service; all those journeyings of his ending in nothing but trade with the savage tribes. . . . Content with the profits accruing from this trade, that officer was very slack in pursuing the discovery which ought to have been the principal object of his efforts."[43]

In 1744 La Vérendrye was forced to retire as commandant of the Posts of the Western Sea. He left the west an embittered man. His "zeal," he wrote, was "a matter of ridicule." "If debts . . . of more than forty thousand livres are an advantage, I can flatter myself that I am very rich, and if I had gone on I should have become richer still."[44]

The opening words of La Vérendrye's letter to Beauharnois telling of a trip west in 1738–39. "I had the honor, Monsieur," he begins, "last year to inform you of my departure from Michilimackinac with six canoes carrying twenty-two men, equipped in such a way as to travel fast."

Five years later administrations changed, and La Vérendrye was reappointed to his post in the west. Zeal restored, he submitted a plan proposing to discover the western sea via the Saskatchewan River. Had he done it, he might have stumbled on the headwaters of the Columbia River, as David Thompson was to do more than fifty years later. But he died before he could set out and never got a chance to prove that his last scheme could have worked.[45]

The years 1740–45 were the height of the French fur trade, and a heavy traffic passed over the Grand Portage. A lease to conduct trade in the posts of "La Mer de l'Ouest" went for eight thousand livres, but the cost did not stop the merchants. In 1740 one sent five canoes and thirty-two men through Grand Portage, and in 1743 another sent eight canoes and fifty-eight men. In the lists of voyageurs engaged for La Mer de l'Ouest in the 1750s, one can find many names that would stay prominent in the fur trade for years: Parrenteau, Forcier, Gauthier, Landry, Charbonneau, and Laplante, to name a few.[46]

Despite all this activity, neither archaeology nor documentary research has proved whether the French built a post at Grand Portage. In 1936 archaeologists found traces of a building, measuring about eighteen by thirty feet and oriented north-south, constructed in the French style in the center of the palisaded area. No datable artifacts were found, however, and subsequent excavations did not reveal the location of the structure. If it was a French building, it probably looked like the "Hogstye" of a post the Hudson's Bay Company emissary Anthony Henday came across on the Saskatchewan in 1754–55. "It is 26 feet long; 12 feet wide; 9 feet high to the ridge; having a sloping roof; the Walls Log on Log; the top covered with Birch-rind, fastened together with willows, & divided into three apartments: One for Trading goods, one for Furs, and the third they dwell in." The courtly commandant of this log hut gave the visiting Briton a chivalrous welcome. He was, Henday said, "dressed very Genteel, but the men wear nothing but thin drawers, & striped cotton shirts ruffled at the hands and breast." There was "a good deal of Bowing and Scraping between us."[47]

French trading practices had matured over the years and by now contrasted markedly with those of their English rivals. At the posts on Hudson Bay, the Indians were not allowed into the forts but were forced to trade through a window. "Fraternizing" was strictly forbidden. The French had learned by painful experience to base their system on accommodation to Indian institutions. "It is surprising to observe what an influence the French have over the Natives," Henday reported back to Hudson Bay. They "talk Several [Indian] Languages to perfection: they have the advantage of us in every shape; and if they had Brazile tobacco, which they

Archaeologists provide one source of information about life at Grand Portage. This broken case bottle, recovered at the site of Fort Charlotte in 1963, is one of the few objects found from the period of the French fur trade.

Hand-painted French faïence plate found at Fort Charlotte. The verse reads: "At the bottom of my bottle / I imprison love / For the juice of the grape / Makes my heart burn with passion."

have not, would entirely cut off our trade." Another Hudson's Bay Company official admitted that the French ascendancy was due to "kind offices and liberality in dealing, which we think of no consequence."[48]

Of course, not every Frenchman got along this well in Indian country. La Vérendrye's replacement, Jacques le Gardeur, sieur de St. Pierre, passed across the Grand Portage in 1751 and found little good to say about the country. "This route is of the most difficult nature," he wrote. "Great experience is necessary to know the roads. Bad as I had imagined them, I was surprised at the reality." Though he was "very well received" by the Indians, he found them "unsettled and very impertinent," with a "want of subordination" due to the "too great indulgence with which they have been treated." He sent an ensign to outdo La Vérendrye by founding a fort near present Calgary, in the very shadow of the Rocky Mountains —the farthest west the French ventured. But the outpost was soon abandoned, and St. Pierre passed along his command to the Chevalier de La Corne.[49]

It became La Corne's duty to preside over the final French withdrawal from the west. In 1754 war broke out between the French, English, and Indians on the Ohio frontier. The French and Indian War soon engulfed the colonies of both European powers, then merged into the greater conflict of the Seven Years' War in Europe. The battle lines in America paralleled older Indian conflicts—the Algonquians sided with the French and the Iroquois with the English. In 1755 La Corne closed up the posts of La Mer de l'Ouest, and by 1759 all of Lake Superior was officially abandoned. The fort at Kaministikwia was destroyed by fire, and the forty-ton ship that had plied the waters of Lake Superior was sunk.[50]

France had need of its allies, for the war was mainly decided by Indian armies. François de La Vérendrye, a son of Pierre, came back to raise troops among the tribes of Lake Superior. The Ojibway, loyal to the French and alarmed at the prospect of a British-Iroquois takeover, responded. The war leader Mamongeseda, whose father had come from the Caribou clan at Grand Portage, led a party of Ojibway who fought alongside the Marquis de Montcalm on the Plains of Abraham in 1759. But their efforts were not enough. Quebec fell, then Montreal. In 1760 the French surrendered, and in the 1763 Treaty of Paris, they ceded Canada to British control.[51]

# CHAPTER THREE

# Across the Divide

A little west of Grand Portage lies the height of land dividing the waters of the Great Lakes from those flowing to Hudson Bay. The voyageurs had a custom when they passed over the divide. Any man in the canoe brigade who had never crossed that way before was "baptised." A clerk named John Macdonell went through the ceremony in 1793.

> *I was instituted a* North man *by* Batême *[baptism] performed by sprinkling water in my face with a small cedar Bow dipped in a ditch of water and accepting certain conditions such as not to let any new hand pass by that road without experiencing the same ceremony which stipulates particularly never to kiss a voyageur's wife against her own free will the whole being accompanied by a dozen of Gun shots fired one after another in an Indian manner. The intention of this Batême being only to claim a glass. I complied with the custom and gave the men . . . a two gallon keg.[1]*

Most fur traders thought little of it, but the ceremony enacted a symbolic rebirth. The divide was more than a geographical barrier—it separated two profoundly different worlds. One could not enter the west and come back unchanged. Crossing over was a watershed in most traders' lives, the point where they left home and eastern conventions behind.

In the late eighteenth century Grand Portage was the site of a schism between cultures, as British capitalism met the alien values of wintering traders whose lives had been changed by Indian tribes and their values.

## Greedy and Needy Adventurers

More than land, the British inherited from the French a potential network of alliances with Indian tribes. It was only potential, though. The French had surrendered in 1760, but the English had neglected to conclude peace with their allies, the Indian tribes. Inexperienced traders started blundering west before they realized that the war was not yet over.

A twenty-two-year-old New Jerseyan named Alexander Henry was one of the first. Later called "the handsome Englishman" by the Indians, he was "about the middle size, distinguished by an easy and dignified deportment." He was candid, open, friendly—and blessed with as many lives as a cat. He would need them all. In 1761, he wrote, "proposing to avail myself of the new market, which was thus thrown open to British adventure, I . . . procured a quantity of goods" and set out for the west. "I was altogether a stranger to the commerce in which I was engaging." With foresight, he

Alexander Henry

stopped in Canada to hire an experienced man, Etienne Campion, to teach him the ropes.[2]

On the way west, Indians repeatedly warned Henry not to risk his life among the Ojibway, fast allies of the French. By the time he took them seriously, he didn't have enough supplies to turn back. So he disguised himself as a voyageur and let Campion pass for the proprietor. No one was fooled. When he arrived at the Ojibway town of Michilimackinac where Lakes Michigan and Huron meet, Henry found himself thrust into international diplomacy.

Mihnehwehna—the tall, imposing chief of the Michilimackinac Ojibway—met him in a council. "Looking steadfastly at me, where I sat in ceremony, with an interpreter on either hand, [he observed] that the English . . . were brave men, and not afraid of death, since they dared to come, as I had done, fearlessly among their enemies." Then, as the young fur trader "inwardly endured the tortures of suspense," Mihnehwehna spoke:

> *Englishman, you know that the French king is our father. He promised to be such; and we, in return, promised to be his children. —This promise we have kept. . . . You are his enemy. . . . You know that his enemies are ours. . . .*
>
> *Englishman, although you have conquered the French, you have not yet conquered us! We are not your slaves. These lakes, these woods and mountains, were left to us by our ancestors. They are our inheritance; and we will part*

The importance of ceremony in relations between Indians and Europeans is evident in Peter Rindisbacher's depiction of a British officer saying farewell to his Indian allies after a battle at Prairie du Chien during the War of 1812.

*with them to none. Your nation supposes that we, like the white people, cannot
live without bread—and pork—and beef! But, you ought to know, that He, the
Great Spirit and Master of Life, has provided food for us, in these spacious
lakes, and on these woody mountains.*

*Englishman, our father, the king of France, employed our young men to
make war upon your nation. In this warfare, many of them have been killed; and
it is our custom to retaliate, until such time as the spirits of the slain are satisfied. . . .*

*Englishman, your king has never sent us any presents, nor entered into
any treaty with us, wherefore he and we are still at war.*

Lucid as this explanation of the Ojibway position was, it gave little com-
fort to Henry. In the end, however, Mihnehwehna decided that "you have
ventured your life among us, in the expectation that we should not molest
you. You do not come armed, with an intention to make war; you come in
peace, to trade with us. . . . We shall regard you, therefore, as a brother; and
you may sleep tranquilly."

Much relieved, Henry "assorted my goods, and hired Canadian interpreters and clerks, in whose care I was to send them . . . into Lake Superi-
or, among the Chipeways, and to the Grand Portage, for the north-west."
His men may have been among those who spent the winter at Rainy Lake.
Meanwhile, a detachment of Rogers' Rangers arrived at Michilimackinac
to "take possession" for the British, as they thought. This controversial
corps of British-American frontiersmen was under the command of Robert
Rogers, a swashbuckling war hero. The Indians allowed them to stay. The
next spring the soldiers escorted a brigade of traders to Grand Portage,
already the gateway for a growing British trade.[3]

But the fur trade was on shaky foundations. By 1763 the English government still had not "covered the bodies of the dead"—the Indian custom
of paying restitution for casualties in war, a step necessary for peace. No
councils had been held, no diplomatic relations established. Led by an Ottawa named Pontiac, the Great Lakes tribes decided to drive the British
back by a series of simultaneous attacks on western posts. The Ojibway
captured Michilimackinac, and Alexander Henry barely escaped death by
hiding in the attic of a French Canadian. After a series of hair's-breadth es-
capes, Henry was rescued by an Ojibway adoptive relative. Other fur
traders were not so lucky.

In 1764 the British finally caught on. They sent ambassadors through the
Great Lakes suing for peace. A huge council and feast were held at Niagara.
One of the Lake Superior Ojibway in attendance asked eloquently "to have
liberty to trade as formerly."[4]

The next year Alexander Henry emerged as kingpin of the Lake Superior trade. He formed a partnership with a longtime trader, Jean Baptiste Cadotte, who had saved his life during Pontiac's War. Theirs was typical of many partnerships springing up, combining French-Canadian experience with British capital. Henry managed to get a monopoly of the Lake Superior trade and sent four canoes and twelve men west. Without competition, he was able to charge exorbitant prices—ten beaver-skins for a blanket, two for a pound of powder, two for an ax, one for a knife, and twenty for a gun. All his accounts were kept in beavers.[5]

But the days of the old monopoly system were numbered. New ideas were abroad in Britain—ideas of free trade, competition, and laissez-faire economics. Modern capitalism was putting down its roots, and the fur trade was one of the first laboratories in which the new theories were tested. In 1766 a traders' petition challenged the government's right to carve up markets and hand them out to whomsoever lobbied and bribed most effectively. Soon the British authorities gave in and threw the trade open to any small businessman who wanted to take the risk.[6]

During the early 1760s Grand Portage was once again a rendezvous site where the Cree and Assiniboine came to pick up trade goods from Ojibway middlemen and the occasional European trader. The Ojibway, the recognized owners of Grand Portage by this date, gladly hosted the festivities. The summer rendezvous was an old Indian tradition that included socializing, marriage, religious observances, dancing, and music as well as trade. By one account, a thousand or more people sometimes gathered at or passed through Grand Portage in summer during these years.[7]

The rendezvous of 1767 was observed by the first visitor to leave an account of Grand Portage—a portly Yankee surveyor named Jonathan Carver. He came as a member of a party sent out from Michilimackinac by Robert Rogers. Officially the group was looking for the Northwest Passage. What it was doing unofficially is less clear, though guesses ranged from inciting the Indian tribes to rebel (unlikely) to trading furs on Rogers's behalf (more likely). Carver was the only one who profited from the expedition. Rogers ended up in jail, accused of treason, while Carver went to London and published a best seller about his trip.

Jonathan Carver

"Arrivd at the Grand Portage," Carver wrote in his diary on July 14, 1767. "Here those who go on the north-west trade . . . carry over their canoes and baggage about nine miles." Carver's party "found the king of the Christenoes [Cree] and several of his people encamped who was glad to see us." The "king," he wrote, was "upwards of sixty years of age, tall and slightly made, but he carried himself very erect. He was of a courteous, affable disposition, and treated me, as did all the chiefs, with great civility." The Cree and some Assiniboine had come "in search of traders from Michilimackinac with a design if possible to git some of them to go into their country and winter with them." During the war they had traded with the Hudson's Bay Company, but Carver found that "these honest people" gave an "extraordinary account" of their bad treatment by the English monopoly. Presciently, he noted that "a factory [trading post] set up at the Great Carrying Place on the north of Lake Superior and well supplyed with articles for the Indian trade would in a little time draw a great part of those innocent people who are thus treated like brutes by the company at Hudson's Bay."[8]

There were more than three hundred people at the rendezvous, and food was scarce. Carver's party "procured some rice of this people and a plenty of fish. Otherwise we must have starvd to death." Even so, the explorers waited uneasily for a shipment of supplies from Rogers at Michilimackinac, fearing "a mutiny would break out among the people which

Flags and medals were official gifts given to Indian leaders by their European allies. This British flag, which was made about 1815, together with an older British flag and two silver peace medals, belonged to the May-mushkowaush family of Grand Portage for many generations.

George III's likeness appears on this 1814 silver peace medal, with the royal coat of arms on the reverse side. The Ojibway family that owned the flags and peace medals presented them to the Minnesota Historical Society in 1979.

we expected every day on account of our being in want of provision."[9]

They spent the time in councils, smoking pipes and exchanging presents. The Indians gave furs and the commander of Carver's party gave a "stand of colours" (flag) to the "chief of the carrying-place." Carver mentioned no traders' buildings, but there were fourteen or fifteen Cree dwellings and a "large house" built by the Ojibway—at one point he even called it a "castle." It may have been fortified with palisades to protect it from attack by the Dakota.

In August some French-Canadian traders finally arrived, bringing the anxious explorers letters from Rogers. To their dismay, he ordered them on to the Pacific but provided no supplies. Sensibly, Carver and his party decided to give up. They never made it across the portage.

Mike Flatte, member of the Grand Portage Indian band in the 1920s, holding one of the British flags that had been passed down in his family; he is wearing the peace medals around his neck.

Many others did. In 1767 fourteen canoe crews carried £5,117 of goods through Grand Portage, and that fall just three companies sent back 4,293 beaver pelts. Some of the traders were old-timers like François Le Blanc, Maurice Blondeau, and Alexander Henry's mentor Etienne Campion. But there were newcomers, too. James Finlay, who wintered on the Saskatchewan River in 1768–69, was haughtily dismissed by the Hudson's Bay Company as "an illitterate [sic] person entirely unacquainted with Geography." Thomas Corry may have been on the Red River as early as 1766. Collectively, they were known to the English monopoly as "pedlars."[10]

But like Alexander Henry, the peddlers were often ignorant of the Indian common-law practices regarding trade. One such practice, known well to the French in the early days, held that anyone traveling through the territory of another tribe had "certain rights to pay in the places of passage." The Ojibway on the lakes west of Grand Portage wanted trade goods and were angered when traders passed through their land to reach the Assiniboine and Cree. In 1765 they began to assert their right to control the flow of traffic.[11]

This was sometimes done in a polite and formal way. When traders arrived at an Ojibway village, they were first greeted with "ceremonious presents" intended to establish a cordial relationship. The presents, mainly food, were placed in a heap; then the trader was summoned and addressed in a speech. Trade rhetoric had not changed much since La Vérendrye's day. According to Alexander Henry, "They tell him, that the Indians are happy in seeing him return to their country; that they have been long in expectation of his arrival; that their wives have deprived themselves of their provisions, in order to afford him a supply; that they are in great want, being destitute of every thing." The trader was then expected to return a handsome present and give them goods on credit.[12]

But if the trader refused to cooperate, or tried to pass through without stopping, the speeches got more hostile. When Henry made such a mistake, one chief reminded him "that we must be well aware of his power to prevent our going further; that if we passed now, he could put us all to death on our return; and that under these circumstances, he expected us to be exceedingly liberal in our presents." In essence, they required a toll like the tariffs and excises merchants paid when passing the boundaries of European countries.[13]

But the inexperienced traders saw it otherwise. They indignantly accused the Indians of extortion and plunder. The Rainy Lake Ojibway were branded as "ungovernable and rapacious," and their neighbors on Lake of the Woods came to be known as "Pilleurs," or Pillagers. (The name is still used, proudly, by the Ojibway at Leech Lake.) Even the Hudson's Bay Company heard of the "innumerable hardships which the Pedlers suffer from several Nations of Indians through who they pass in coming up from the grand carrying Place." Traders who could not adapt suffered; those who could, succeeded.[14]

One who succeeded—and paved the way for others—was Thomas Corry. This he did by acting in a seemingly unbusinesslike way. Wintering in the west in 1771–72, he fostered a reputation for hospitality and liberality. "All speak greatly in praise of the generosity of the Chief Pedler Correy," reported the Hudson's Bay Company sourly. He was "giving abundance of goods for nothing, and trading at a cheap rate." Corry particularly focused on a powerful Cree trading captain named Wappenassew, who had been leading his people to Hudson Bay since 1755. Wappenassew "lives in [Corry's] House all the winter, dines at Table with the Master, & his family are cloathed with cloth & no favour is refused." In return, Wappenassew agreed to convoy Corry's canoes past the Ojibway. Corry wrote mockingly to the Hudson's Bay Company that Wappenassew "Desired me to let you know that he Dwoe knot go to See you this Springe But . . . Will go to the Grand-portge with me. . . . [H]e hopes you will knot Bee angre with him." With his reputation for liberality ringing through the west, Corry raked in so many furs he was able to retire in two years. Where sharp dealing, European style, failed, acting with the grain of Indian trade and leadership principles brought success.[15]

By the mid-1770s the traders accepted Ojibway tolls as an established custom, and reports of conflict grew fewer. For their part, many Indians came to prefer the convenience of having peddlers deliver goods to their villages, even though the prices might be higher than those at Hudson Bay. It was a genuinely different kind of transaction than they had known before. The peddlers represented no one but themselves and therefore brought no diplomatic or military connections. Trade became less a matter of formal negotiation between leaders and more of a one-to-one relationship of salesman and customer. Many of the customers were women.[16]

The commerce through Grand Portage was "an object of considerable note" to Canada by 1778, bringing in £40,000 a year and employing about five hundred people. For a month each summer those people congregated at Grand Portage "for the refreshing and comforting [of] those who are employed in the more distant voyages." In about 1768 a trader named Erskine or Askin cleared a site just west of Grand Portage Creek for a post, and soon the traders were said to have "tolerable Houses" along the beachline of the bay, with stockades "to cover them from any insult from the numerous savage tribes, who resort there during that time." Though no descriptions survive, the posts were probably log huts shingled in elm bark, with clay chimneys and doors of untanned hide.[17]

"Amongst so great a number of people not the most moral or enlight-

*Camp Scene at Grand Portage,* 1857, by Eastman Johnson. This artist provided the earliest known views of Grand Portage.

ened," one trader wrote, "it is easy to conceive that there must infallibly be Jarring & disputes." And jarring there was. Grand Portage in these years was described as "a pent-up hornets' nest of conflicting factions intrenched in rival forts." A typical company consisted of a single entrepreneur, backed by a merchant who supplied credit and goods, in charge of as few as three or as many as sixty hired men. Alexander Henry represented one of the larger firms when he arrived in 1775 with sixteen canoes and fifty-two men. He "found the traders in a state of extreme reciprocal hostility, each pursuing his interests in such a manner as might most injure his neighbour." They lured each others' employees away, stole furs owed to other companies, sold liquor, reneged on debts, and generally acted (according to the Hudson's Bay Company) like "wild fellows . . . going about Sword in hand, threatening the Natives to make them trade." It is no wonder that "the winter . . . was one continued scene of disagreements and quarrels."[18]

This was the negative side of the system the British had introduced. But in capitalism, a free market never lasts long. The merchants themselves, who only ten years before had been singing the praises of free enterprise, now preached the evils of competition. It "occasioned such disorder," they said, that it caused "manifest ruin to some of the parties concerned and the destruction of the Trade." Their solution: monopoly.[19]

But not the old style of monopoly granted by the government. Though the most powerful traders lobbied hard to reintroduce such a system, the tenor of the times was against it. The more modern form of monopoly evolved through merger, when companies realized it was in their own interest to cooperate rather than compete. By pooling their resources, they were able to squeeze smaller businessmen out of the market.

Several forces nudged the fur trade toward monopoly. First was the high cost. A great deal of capital was needed for a long term, and few small businessmen could get enough credit. Next were the complex logistics of transportation and supply in the northwest. As journeys stretched far beyond Grand Portage, it became less possible for lone proprietors to manage it all. They needed business managers in the east and depots along the way. And then there was the need for supervision and control of traders in the west. Not only did lawlessness make life unsafe, but traders soon found that their Indian customers "could entertain no respect for persons who had conducted themselves with so much irregularity and deceit."[20]

A number of fluid coalitions formed in the late 1770s. One that prefigured later events came together in 1775. Alexander Henry, with his penchant for being in the right place at the right time, was one member. The others would become key figures in Grand Portage's history.

"An Englishman they call Joe" was how the Hudson's Bay Company first heard of Joseph Frobisher. Everyone called this "kind and friendly" Yorkshireman by his nickname in those days; later he would be "Mr. Frobisher" to the elite of Canada. He was oldest of a trio of brothers who entered the Grand Portage fur trade in 1765. They had been among the rush of traders stopped by the Rainy Lake Ojibway in 1769 but had gotten to Lake Winnipeg the following year. The brothers made a good team. Benjamin was the brains of the enterprise and soon established himself in Montreal, where he handled the administration of the family business. Thomas was a dependable trader. But Joseph was leader in the west. He had managed to lure an experienced Frenchman, Louis Primot, away from the Hudson's Bay Company and with his guidance set up the first post on the Churchill River. The year before Alexander Henry met him, Joseph had spent a nightmarish winter on the Churchill, so starved that when he came crawling back to Cumberland House the Hudson's Bay Company men found the sight "really shocking. One or two of his men dyed for real want, and one of them Shott by the Indians for Eating human flesh, the Corps of one of their deceased friends. Mr. Forborsher himself ware so destresst that he eat . . . many of his Furs." Yet after a trip to Grand Portage for supplies, he gamely headed back west.[21]

Lurid tales also hung around another of the men Henry met that summer of 1775. Peter Pond was a Connecticut native on his first trip to the northwest. He was a loner, eccentric even among frontiersmen. "He thought himself a philosopher," one acquaintance wrote, "and was odd in his manners." His own fancifully spelled memoirs reveal a quarrelsome, shrewd man with a Yankee twang and a keenly satirical sense of humor. Pond had been involved in the fur trade south of the Great Lakes since 1765. While in Detroit he had dueled with another trader and (according to Pond) "the Pore fellow was unfortennt [unfortunate]. I then Came Doan the Cuntrey & Declard the fact But thare was none to Prosacute me." The pattern of violence would be repeated. In 1782 he wintered with Jean Etienne

Waden, a Swiss immigrant with a reputation for "strict probity and known sobriety." As another trader put it, "Two men, of more opposite characters, could not, perhaps, have been found." A quarrel ensued, and Waden was shot. Pond was accused of the murder, but again the courts seem not to have acted. Though free of jail, Pond would never again be free of suspicion.[22]

Despite Pond's dangerous shortcomings as a partner, he was a brilliant explorer. In 1778 a group of traders backed him in an expedition to the fabled far-north realm of Athabasca. There he met tribes that had never had a trader among them. They gave him more furs than he could carry back to Grand Portage. Ever after, Pond felt as if Athabasca belonged to him.[23]

But perhaps the most important member of the 1775 coalition was not even present at Grand Portage. Simon McTavish was one of Pond's financial backers. They may have met in the 1770s when McTavish was getting his start shipping rum from Albany to Detroit. Born in Scotland, McTavish had come to America penniless at age thirteen. Although he claimed to be a devotee of "good wine, good oysters, and pretty girls," business was his true love—not to say obsession. And he excelled at it. A visitor to Montreal in 1804 wrote that the masterful McTavish was "entirely unequalled here in acuteness and reach of thought"; other associates gave him the derisive nickname "Marquis" for his domineering manner. In an era when most merchants were investing in the trade southwest of Lake Superior, McTavish turned his prodigious energy north to the Grand Portage trade. About 1774 he and a partner bought a "perriauger"—a wooden canoe—to ship furs between the portage and Sault Ste. Marie. He whisked from Montreal to Grand Portage to Albany to London—but never once west of Grand Portage. Though he would become the mastermind behind the North West Company, he never dealt with an Indian for furs.[24]

With cooperation breaking out all over, the 1775–76 season was very profitable for the traders. Henry and the Frobishers brought back more than twelve thousand beaver skins, and McTavish's associates secured £15,000 worth of furs. But when Henry came to Lake of the Woods on his way down, he heard disturbing rumors. The Indians told him that "some strange nation had entered Montréal, taken Québec, killed all the English, and would certainly be at the Grand Portage before we arrived there." It was the *Bastonnais*, they said—the Bostonians. It was only too true. War had broken out again, this time between Britain and the American colonies.[25]

The fur trade had a lot to do with the war. Ever since 1763 it had been British policy to protect the lands and sovereignty of the Indian tribes west of the Appalachians from encroachment by American colonists. The British did so for the sake of Canada's economy. That colony's largest industry was the fur trade, which depended on preservation of the wilderness and the Indian hunting culture. When the Quebec Act of 1774 set aside the Ohio frontier for the use of traders and Indians, the Americans were outraged. One of the freedoms they fought for in their revolution was the freedom to take Indian land and destroy Indian life-styles.[26]

The Bastonnais never made it to Grand Portage, but the Redcoats did. In 1778 a number of traders petitioned the government of Canada to send troops to protect their investments during the summer rendezvous. Their request had more to do with labor problems, however, than marauding rebels. They wanted the troops to enforce voyageur contracts and payment of debts, track down "canoe men who have run away from their masters," and take over the expensive diplomatic duty of "giving colours and other marks of distinction" to the Indians. The government, on its side, was suspicious about the quantities of guns, ammunition, and blankets being shipped to Grand Portage, which might easily find their way into the wrong hands. To keep an eye on all this, it agreed to send an officer and twelve men from the King's Eighth Regiment of Foot.[27]

A consortium of traders furnished the soldiers with canoe transportation, a guide named "Big Charlie," and accommodations at the portage. By this time at least one trader lived on the bay year round. John Askin, a Michilimackinac merchant, instructed his clerk at Grand Portage, Joseph Beausoleil, to "have a house ready" for the soldiers "which they can use until able to provide for themselves. It should have a chimney. Also be so good as to have your men prepare 200 pickets, 14 feet in length, and have them put on the beach between the old fort and yours."[28]

In May 1778 Lieutenant Thomas Bennett, one other officer, five soldiers, and seven canoemen set out from Michilimackinac. They brought two small cannons, gunpowder for ceremonial salutes, and carpentry tools for erecting a fort—plus dry goods, tobacco, and one hundred gallons of rum "to enable [Bennett] to receive the visits from the Indians." The summer passed placidly. The soldiers began the erection of a small fort and cleared a road (the site of neither is known). The fort was still unfinished when they left in August, expecting to return the next year. But by 1779 soldiers were needed elsewhere, and the troops never made it back.[29]

This halfhearted show of military muscle was by no means the most important impact the American Revolution had on the Grand Portage fur trade. As the Great Lakes region became embroiled in war, commerce shifted north and Grand Portage's share increased. But the trade, up to now almost free of regulation, began to labor under wartime restrictions. The British military commanders, believing that fur traders were basically a pack of "greedy and needy adventurers," would have liked to shut them out altogether. But they did not dare—partly because furs were "the staple trade of this Province," pumping £200,000 into Montreal's economy, and partly because the officials feared alienating the powerful western tribes,

Brass button from the uniform of a British King's Eighth Regiment soldier. The button was found by archaeologists at the site of Fort Charlotte.

whose military aid might be crucial in the war. So they satisfied themselves with regulations. All private shipping on the Great Lakes was banned, and traders were required to transport goods via military vessels—an unreliable solution that produced more than one gray hair. In 1778 the military capriciously blocked food shipments, raising the specter that "some of the People in the Back Country in all probability will perish for want." The next year the licenses were issued so late that the goods could not reach the west.[30]

The effect was to consolidate the trade in the hands of a few Montreal merchants. With the Great Lakes closed off, American traders—among them Simon McTavish—had to move to Montreal to stay in business. In 1779 representatives of nine Montreal companies met at Grand Portage and agreed to pool their resources. Although this one-year partnership was considered "little better than an armed truce," it was the nucleus around which the North West Company would form. Between them, the Frobisher brothers and McTavish controlled a quarter of the shares. That proportion would grow.[31]

It was during the American Revolution that the fur trade achieved the organization that would characterize it for the next twenty years. Later, the system would become more elaborate and the jobs more specialized, but the underlying division of responsibilities was between the merchant and the winterer.

### "This adventurous Traffick"

The separate jobs of merchant and winterer originated in the French era as a practical necessity—given the distances and slowness of travel, no one per-

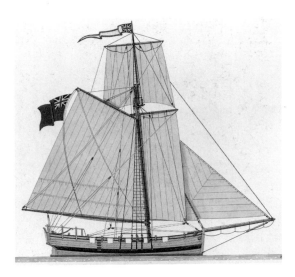

The sloop *Welcome*, an armed ship that carried fur trade goods on the lower Great Lakes during the American Revolution. Similar ships were used on Lake Superior.

son could handle every aspect of the business. But as the British refined the system, the differences between the two sets of men grew. The jobs required talents so different and produced experiences so alien to one another that two distinct "job cultures" began to evolve.

The Montreal merchants needed skills in administration, supervision, finance, and marketing. Because Canada had few industries of its own, almost all goods had to be imported. The merchant was in touch with an exporting house in London that purchased specialized goods designed for the Indian trade from around the world. The tobacco came from Brazil via Portugal, the beads came from Venice or Holland, vermilion from China, knives from Sheffield, and cloth from Leeds and Manchester. The Montreal merchant placed his orders in the fall. The goods were packed, insured, and shipped the next spring. They arrived in Montreal in June, too late to go west that year. The merchant stored some of the goods in his capacious warehouses and sent others out to be "made up" into articles desired by the Indians. He hired seamstresses to sew cotton into shirts, wool into leggings, blankets into capotes. Silversmiths created beaver pendants, armbands, gorgets, and brooches.[32]

By early spring, everything had to be ready for the merchant's employees to start packing up the lighter goods for shipment west. Packing was a skilled job. Bales could not weigh more than ninety pounds. They had to be watertight and contain a variety of merchandise so that one or two could be lost without disaster. Meanwhile, the merchant was hiring canoemen and guides in the rural French-Canadian communities around Montreal. He was purchasing special freight canoes made in Trois Rivières and arranging cargo space on ships that went via the Great Lakes. Everything had to be ready by May, when the ice broke and ships and canoe brigades set off for Grand Portage. From that point on, all were racing the clock. They had only five months before ice set in again.

Transportation west of Montreal was the merchant's largest single cost, accounting for about half the year's investment. It was mainly a labor expense. The canoes went via the portage-strewn Ottawa River, a route Benjamin Frobisher called "eminently dangerous. . . . [I]t is [due] to [the voyageurs'] dexterity alone and the knowledge they have of the management of Canoes . . . that so few accidents happen." A canoeload of goods worth £500 at Montreal was worth £750 at Grand Portage, just from transportation expense. It was cheaper to send goods by ship via the Great Lakes, and many heavy and bulky items went that way. But ships were subject to government regulations, were slower, and were less likely to arrive on schedule—and timing was everything in the fur trade. So the canoes continued to go.

One of the merchant's main logistical problems was feeding his employees on the way to Grand Portage. Each canoe set off from Montreal with about a thousand pounds of biscuit, pork, and peas, which lasted only as far as Michilimackinac. There, new supplies had to be waiting. Ships brought flour and corn from Detroit. The Ottawa and Ojibway who farmed on the shores of Lake Michigan sold huge quantities of corn, beans, and maple sugar to provisioning agents at Michilimackinac, who supplied the northwest brigades. Shipments of food also had to be waiting at Grand Portage or there would be mutiny.[33]

Ship cargoes, canoe brigades, provisions, and everything else had to converge on Grand Portage in early July, when the people from inland began to arrive. The merchants had two weeks to get everything over the portage. Without telephones, reliable mail, or motor transportation, the logistics must have been a nightmare. Benjamin Frobisher said only that it required "the utmost dispatch."[34]

After the busy weeks at Grand Portage, the merchant still couldn't relax. Furs were perishable and had to get to England that year. Wolf, moose, and other heavy hides could go east via ship, but fine furs went by canoe. In Montreal they were sorted and graded, then insured and placed on ships for England, where they were auctioned the following spring. The merchant had to keep abreast of the varying prices. Since many furs were reexported to Russia, France, and Holland, tariffs and wars had a major effect on the market. Payment for the furs did not reach Montreal until May or June.[35]

The merchant got no return on the goods he had sent west until the following year. From ordering to getting a return took almost four years. This turnaround time drove out small businessmen faster than anything else. The merchant had to be his own banker. Although the whole structure was built on borrowed money—the London exporter gave credit to the merchant, the merchant to the winterer, the winterer to the Indian—most bills came due in a year, and returns took longer. It is no wonder Benjamin Frobisher called the business "precarious," or that another trader, John Inglis, described it with understatement as "this adventurous Traffick."[36]

And, of course, nothing ever went as planned. The ships needed repairs or were late, orders got lost, people failed to deliver goods and food as promised. Canoes were wrecked, taxes increased, war inevitably broke out somewhere. It was a business no sane person would invest a penny in.

But as any investment advisor will say, a great risk may carry the potential for great profit. Because of their control over so many aspects of the trade, the merchants could (and did) pass on their expenses and risk to their hapless partners in the field, to their young clerks, and even to the voyageurs. They sat at the center of the immense web of trade relations, pulling strings in London, Montreal, and Grand Portage. The ones whose capital and organization did not fail eventually became "a kind of commercial aristocracy, living in lordly and hospitable style." In Montreal they "took the lead in all assemblies, clubs, and other circles of society: their name influenced the tone of public opinion." They were among the most powerful men in Canada.[37]

While the merchants were risking their money, the winterers in the field were all too often risking their lives. Many of their business skills were interpersonal ones derived from years of experience. Winterers were trained through a long apprenticeship in the ways of Indian diplomacy and trade. The ones who adapted best succeeded. This made their skills seem less valuable to the outside world, and their rewards were less than those of their merchant partners. Many winterers dreamed of earning enough to move to Montreal and become a merchant; only a very few ever did.

Once past Grand Portage, the winterer entered a world where he and his men were entirely dependent upon the Indians who made the canoes they traveled in, provided the food they ate, guided them, interpreted for them, and shared geographical knowledge. The Indians picked sites for their posts, made their snowshoes and moccasins—and hunted, trapped, and cured the skins that the traders sought. Almost all communication and news came through tribespeople, who often kept traders in the dark about competitors' prices and practices. In fact, the Indians constantly used the traders' dependence to assert control over commerce.

One of the winterer's main worries, like the merchant's, was transportation. The brigades left Grand Portage in July and had to reach their wintering spots—some of them two thousand miles distant—before the rivers froze in October. As Benjamin Frobisher admitted, the travelers "are exposed to every misery that it is possible to survive." There were "strains, ruptures, and injuries for life" incurred in portaging. There were terrifying canoe accidents. Loss of life became so routine that traders who had seen it over and over made calm notations like, "lost two men and eleven pieces of goods."[38]

The worst hardship was lack of provisions. Though the canoes set out one-third full of food, it soon ran out and "they must and always do, depend on the Natives . . . for an Additional Supply." At Rainy Lake the traders bought wild rice and fish from the Ojibway; at Lake Winnipeg they could get pemmican. This mixture of buffalo meat and grease was purchased in huge quantities from Plains Indian women and shipped north to depots along the trade routes. One trader testified that "without this provision, which could not be obtained in any other part of the Country, [we] would be compelled to abandon the most lucrative part of the Trade."[39]

Once at his wintering post, the trader advanced goods to the Indians who came in, then sat down to wait for spring, when the trappers would come back with their furs. Most of the winterer's time was spent in excruciating boredom. "I rise with the sun," trader Angus Shaw wrote to a friend, "and, after *debarbouilling mon visage* [shaving], I take a walk to my traps, return to the house, eat *Tollibees* [a fish] about nine; then take another walk or work all day at something or other. About 7 p.m., I again eat *tollibee* boiled or roasted and pass the rest of the evening in reading or writing. When Indians are about the house I, of course, attend to the interests of my employers. Indeed, my dear man, I find time very long, which I fear may affect my constitution; but there is no help to it."[40]

Some of the winterers played the violin, gardened in spring, and read romances or travel books, dreaming about people doing really adventurous things. Others succumbed to depression, dwelling morbidly on how they were *"self-banished* in this dreary Country an[d] at such a great distance from all I hold dear in this World." To relieve the monotony, the men regularly celebrated holidays "as is usual for them, that is in drinking & fighting." They went to visit other posts even in the most dangerous subzero weather, just for some conversation. The trip to Grand Portage was so much the high point of the year that they began thinking about it in January. "I am fully bent on going down," one wrote a friend. "I think it unpardonable in any man to remain in this country who can afford to leave it."[41]

And yet, year after year, they went back—for during the long, slow months of winter an alchemy took place. Every year a few of the men who went in for the money, fully expecting to return, became absorbed by a culture whose slow rhythms and nonmaterial values took over their minds and hearts.

One who recorded such a transition was a young man from an evangelical Christian family named Daniel Williams Harmon. He set out from

Vermont for Grand Portage in 1800, when he was twenty-two, spurred by his "roving disposition" and by "hopes of gaining a little Gold." It was nineteen years before he returned east.[42]

At first Harmon was repelled by fur trade life. Accustomed to strict observance of the Sabbath, he was shocked to see men playing cards, dancing, and conducting business on Sunday. They "lay aside the most of Christian and Civilized regulations," he accused, "and behave but little better than the Savages themselves." Even his *bourgeois,* whom he admired, "gives in too much to the ways and customs of the Country he is in." For his own part, Harmon read the Bible and prayed to return home unchanged.

Daniel Williams Harmon

He had come west full of prejudice about Indians, and his first contacts with them were contentious. After refusing some men a gift—not realizing he was spurning their oldest customs—he concluded that *"their* fondness for our property and *our* eagerness to obtain their Furs" was "all the friendship that exists between the Traders and Savages of this Country."[43]

But gradually he began to adapt. He learned to smoke a friendly pipe with his customers, to be generous and not grasping. The real change started when he went *en dérouine*—to visit the Indians in their villages. Once, after a long trip by dogsled, he arrived late and half frozen at a cozy Indian lodge. The woman of the family told him to "remain quiet & smoak" by the fire while she unharnessed his dogs and fed them. Though it was near midnight, people all over the village rose to invite him to their homes to eat. At last he bedded down under a warm buffalo robe. "We met with more real politeness (in this way) than is often shown to Strangers in the civilized part of the World, and much more than I had expected [to] meet with from *Savages* as the Indians are generally called, but I think wrongly."

He began to find interest in the change of the seasons, the wildlife, and Indian horticulture and cooking. He even became interested in their religion, writing respectfully of their reverence and sacrifices and admitting they might "believe rightly." But he still couldn't adapt in one way—sexual mores. All around him, traders were marrying Indian and mixed-blood women *à la façon du pays*—according to the custom of the country. There were many practical advantages to it: a wife gave a trader family ties in the Indian community and a partner who knew the crafts, language, and customs. In 1802 a Cree chief offered Harmon his daughter. "He almost persuaded me to accept of her, for I was sure that while I had the Daughter I should not only have the Fathers hunts but those of his relations also, of course [this] would be much in the favor of the Company." He also admitted "a little natural inclination" which "was nigh making me commit another folly, if not a sin,—but thanks be to God alone if I have not been brought into a snare laid no doubt by the Devil himself." Harmon remained chaste.[44]

Three years later it was a different story. When a fourteen-year-old mixed-blood girl was offered him he gave it "mature consideration" and "finally concluded it would be best to accept of her, as it is customary for all the Gentlemen who come in this Country . . . to have a *fair* Partner. . . . When I return to my native land [I] shall endeavour to place her into the hands of some good honest Man, with whom she can pass the remainder of her Days in this Country." But this resolution, like others, gradually faded. At first, Harmon could not think of her as his wife. When their son was born in 1807 she was "the Woman who remains with me." By 1810 she was "my Woman." By 1819 she was "the mother of my children," and parting with her was unthinkable. One of his last diary entries showed what kind of man he had become: "I now pass a short time every day, very pleasantly, teaching my little daughter Polly to read and spell words in the English language. . . . In conversing with my children, I use entirely the Cree, Indian language; with their mother I more frequently employ the French." When eventually he did return east he took his family with him, but he found it impossible to stay and moved back west till age forced him to retire from the trader's life.

Harmon, like many another winterer, had been appropriated by the land where he lived. It now seemed senseless to him how "we are continually harassing and teasing ourselves in hopes of gaining Masses of Silver and Gold"—an attitude diametrically opposed to the capitalist goals of self-interest and accumulation of wealth. He had concluded that "a person . . . *can* be as *virtuous* in this as in any other part of the World." Winterers like Harmon absorbed Indian values into their own belief systems. Some formed a new blend so thorough that they came to feel out of place in their boyhood culture. One, in deciding not to write the son of an old friend in the east, said, "I am an Indian, he is a Christian, he will not like such a rough correspondent." To these men, and even more to their children who followed them into the business, the fur trade was a way of life, a family tradition, an adopted culture—not a business ruled by balance sheets and bills. Old traders often died in what eastern friends considered "poverty and obscurity," but surrounded by large, loyal families. Today, their descendants are often found on reservations, where the generous values they learned from the Indians survive.[45]

The merchant and the winterer were the two types of men who met each year during the rendezvous at Grand Portage. Each depended on the other. But there was also a rift between them that grew larger as the years progressed. They were from opposite sides of the divide.

# CHAPTER FOUR

# The Hurly-Burly of Business

The early 1780s brought two events that would have a profound effect on the history of Grand Portage.

In 1781 and 1782, one of the worst epidemics in North American history swept across the western half of the continent. It was smallpox. The horror of it was still fresh for traders who wrote years after: it "spread its destructive and desolating power, as the fire consumes the dry grass of the field. The fatal infection spread around with a baneful rapidity which no flight could escape. . . . It destroyed . . . whole families and tribes."[1]

The disease seems to have started on the Missouri River and spread north and west till it decimated the population as far as Athabasca. The casualty rate was higher than the Black Death in Europe—most estimates said two-thirds of the population died. Whole villages stood deserted. Hungry dogs mauled the corpses, for no one was left to bury them. One fur trader who went west that year first learned of the tragedy when he met a few survivors who were "in such a state of despair and despondence that they could hardly converse with us. . . . We proceeded up the River with heavy hearts. . . . When we arrived at the House instead of a crowd of Indians to welcome us, all was solitary silence, our hearts failed us."[2]

The population of northern Minnesota did not escape. Ojibway tradition says that a war party of Cree, Assiniboine, and Ojibway went to attack a village on the Missouri River but found it inhabited only by the dead. They brought the disease back to the Red River, from which it spread to Rainy Lake, then to Grand Portage, and south to Leech and Sandy lakes. Years later a traveler in this region commented, "This great extent of country was formerly very populous, but [now] the aggregate of its inhabitants does not exceed three hundred warriors; and, among the few whom I saw, it appeared to me that the widows were more numerous than the men."[3]

It would be hard to overstate the effect of the epidemic on Indian society. Craft techniques died with the artisans; with the elders went medicine knowledge, tribal history, religious traditions, stories, and songs. The political structure faltered when clan leaders died. People left without families had no one to protect them, and in the decades following, reports of domestic violence and murder became more common.[4]

At the time and ever since, the Indians suspected that the whites had introduced the disease deliberately. Such biological warfare had been practiced by the British during the French and Indian War. But in this case it seems unlikely. The fur trade was entirely dependent on Indian hunters and artisans. Traders were salesmen, and it was against their interest to kill their customers. In fact, the Hudson's Bay Company belatedly sponsored a vaccination program, but it did little good. There was a precipitous decline in fur returns in 1782–83. But though traders may not have been responsible, they did not hesitate to take grisly advantage of the situation. At least one of them stole beaver-pelt shrouds from corpses and collected skins offered up as sacrifices.[5]

Smallpox changed the demographic ratio of whites to Indians, and the balance of power shifted. Hitherto, traders had been guests in a thriving society with its own systems of justice and control. Now, with Indian society reeling, the traders unleashed their own sense of justice and hierarchy. Duncan McGillivray, one of the fur trade's autocratic upper class, set the tone. He wanted to see the Indians "dependent; and consequently industrious & subordinate." The trade, which in many ways had reached a mutually beneficial balance, began to show signs of exploitation and domination.[6]

## Lords of the Lakes and Forests

The second important—and not unrelated—event of the 1780s was the founding of the North West Company.

Actually, the kernel of the company had existed since 1775, and the name was even used by various annual mergers that formed throughout the late 1770s. Some historians have picked the coalition of 1779 as the founding. Others name the one of 1782. But the participants themselves often pointed to 1784. Unlike the 1779 agreement, which was formed in summer at Grand Portage, this one was hatched in January, in Montreal—meaning that it was the brainchild of Montreal merchants rather than wintering traders. The center of power had shifted.[7]

The seal of the North West Company

The structure of the company would have given a modern corporate lawyer nightmares. It was never a single corporation, but a loose association of companies. The best modern term is cartel. On the Montreal side

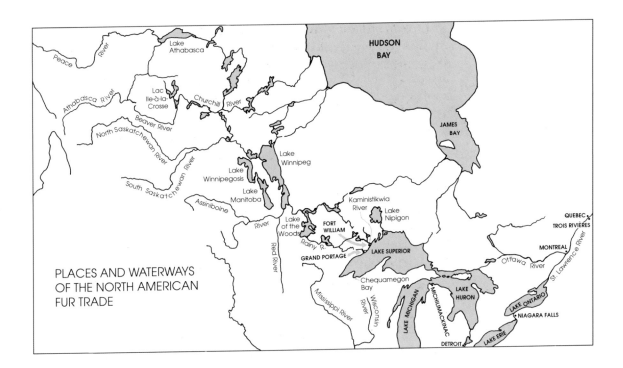

PLACES AND WATERWAYS
OF THE NORTH AMERICAN
FUR TRADE

were the various merchant houses, dominated by the Frobishers and Simon McTavish, each of which received a proportion of the importing and shipping business equal to the number of shares it owned. Each company kept separate books and might deal in other lines of business unrelated to the fur trade. The winterers, instead of being the proprietors of competing companies, became heads of various geographical "departments," each with separate accounts. The departments were so independent that the Montreal partners even charged them separately for interest and shipping. At the end of each yearly agreement the profits were paid out to the shareholders in proportion to their investment, so there was no company treasury.[8]

At first there were sixteen shares, divided between winterers and Montreal agents. But each reorganization gathered more competitors into the fold, and by 1805 there were a hundred shares. One clue to the company's self-image was the fact that it called its fiscal years "adventures." The accounts of each adventure had to be kept separate because the partners were in such a constant state of fratricidal warfare that the company had to be reorganized almost yearly.

Amazingly, it worked. One key was a decision that the partners made in 1787: no share in the company could be sold or granted to anyone but those who had risen through the ranks. Two-thirds of the partners had to approve the new shareholder. This rule strengthened the incentive of the lower-level employees and the camaraderie of the partners. The North West Company became a brotherhood, an exclusive club whose members had all gone past the divide and had their baptism in the ways of the west. They had become "lords of the lakes and forests," in the nostalgic words of Washington Irving. Outsiders often remarked on their *esprit de corps:* "the quiet, inky-fingered clerk of the old [Hudson's Bay] Company, expecting only his poor salary, was no match for the fiery youth who worked on shares."[9]

By 1798 the North West Company employed 50 clerks, 71 interpreter-clerks, 35 guides, and 1,120 canoemen. True to the strict class- and race-consciousness of its founders, the company was a hierarchical organization, but it was a hierarchy that men with the right connections—and the right ethnic background—could climb. At the top were the partners, or *bourgeois,* divided into the Montreal agents and wintering partners. The winterers, each of whom had charge of a district, enjoyed privileges: for example, rations of tea, coffee, and chocolate; a larger allowance of personal belongings; servants or slaves; travel in a "light" canoe set aside for themselves and their baggage. And perhaps the most competed-for, occasional trips back east.[10]

Below the partners were the many "gentlemen" employees who were trying to climb into the ranks of shareholders. A well-educated young man entered the company in his teens or early twenties as a clerk or *commis.* He signed a contract to serve a seven-year apprenticeship in the west for only £100 total and the possibility of getting a share at the end. Some called the seven-year contract "slavery" and "servitude."[11]

Clerks were what most people mean when they say traders. The more experienced, called head clerks, were in charge of individual posts. They kept the accounts and did much of the actual bargaining with the Indians. Yet at the end of their seven years, they often found no shares available. Most opted to stay on at a salary of £100 to £300 a year, still hoping for a partnership, for which "we must depend on success in trade and friends in power." In the closed society of the North West Company, promotion was highly political. In summers when a share became available, Grand Portage was the scene of intense lobbying. Clerks without the right friends or relatives had to wait, sometimes for fifteen or twenty years. They complained bitterly about how promotion was reserved for "dissembling courtiers" rather than hard-working men.

Below the clerks were the clerk-interpreters, often literate mixed-bloods. Most worked on salary, without any expectation of becoming partners. And at the bottom were the illiterate "common laboring men." From the 1780s on, more and more Scots filled the upper echelons, while the lower were open to French Canadians, Iroquois, and mixed-blood Algonquians.

The laborers, too, were divided into ranks. Their canoe skills determined their status. The least skilled were the middlemen (*milieux* in French), who worked in the center of the canoe and carried the goods across portages. Next came the foreman (*avant*) and steersman (*gouvernail*), whose jobs were to direct and steer the vessel and to carry it over portages. Each brigade of four to six canoes had an experienced guide who chose the proper route through the mazy waterways, commanded the canoemen, and was responsible for the vessels and their ladings. Like the captain of a ship, the guide had absolute authority in his sphere—down to countermanding the orders of a *bourgeois*.[12]

The gentlemen of the company looked on the voyageurs with a paternalistic fondness as "common people that must necessarily be employed in the menial offices of this Trade." They freely acknowledged the boatmen's skill—it was astonishing, said one, "to witness the dexterity with which they manage their canoes in those dangerous rapids, carrying them down like lightening [*sic*] on the surface of the water." Most of the gentlemen's praise, however, was reserved for doglike qualities of obedience and mindless endurance—"No men are more submissive to their leaders and employers, more capable of enduring hardship, or more good-humored under priva-

A North canoe on Clove Lake during a 1989 voyageur reenactment

tions. Never are they so happy as when on long and rough expeditions, toiling up river or coasting lakes."[13]

But there was also suspicion, prejudice, and conflict between the classes. "Keep every thing as secret as you can from your men," one *bourgeois* advised an inexperienced clerk; "otherwise these old voyageurs will fish all they know out of your Green Hands." An educated French-Canadian clerk found the laborers' dialect a "barbaric jargon"; some called it *"Français sauvage."* Daniel Harmon wondered, "What conversation would an illiterate ignorant Canadian be able to keep up. All of their chat is about Horses, Dogs, Canoes and Women, and strong Men who can fight a good battle." The voyageurs, he continued, "make very indifferent Companions, and with whom I cannot associate."[14]

The prejudice went both ways, as another young clerk, George Nelson, found when he was injured on his way to Grand Portage from his wintering post. Unable to walk, Nelson was crawling painfully over a portage on hands and knees. "I asked the men to help me, but they refused, cursing me for a damned Englishman and protestant. 'It is good for you' would they repeat with oaths & reproaches & sarcastic Sneers. It irritated me a good deal. I could never divine what could possibly be the cause of this cruel feeling towards me. . . . After many years with them, I at last found it was owing to my nation & my religion."[15]

There might have been other reasons, as well. Like other early extractive industries (lumbering and mining, for example), the fur trade was structured so as to balance the books on the backs of the poorest-paid employees. While wages nominally went up between 1767 and 1800, few workers actually made money, and many ended up owing the company. In 1791 it was said that nine hundred men owed more than ten or fifteen years' pay. They were usually in debt from the moment they started, since they had to borrow from the company for any extra clothing or equipment. The wintering voyageurs were paid once a year at Grand Portage, but they were paid in goods or in vouchers for merchandise from the company-run store. Because of the inflated prices at Grand Portage, the pay was worth only two-thirds of what it would have been in Montreal. In addition, the company made a 50 percent profit on any goods purchased with *bons*. Sales to its own employees were absolutely crucial to the company. "Were it not that the Men Spend their Wages and the extraordinary high price of Bears and Beaver it would be to us a loosing [sic] business," one partner wrote.[16]

In order to make up for exploitative wages, the company allowed workers *permission de porter le pacton*—to trade on their own for relatively worthless pelts like moose and buffalo. Many men earned as much this way as in wages. But there was a catch here, too. When they got to Grand Portage, the only market the men were allowed to sell to was backed by the North West Company itself—and the company made a profit on each transaction.[17]

An incident in 1802 proved how important their employees' business was to the company. An independent firm from Michilimackinac sent a clerk, Paul Hervieux, with a canoeload of goods to trade not with the Indians, but with the voyageurs at the Grand Portage rendezvous. Even before he arrived the partners caught wind of his purpose: "to reduce the prices which the North West Company generally charged there for goods." A rumor said that he boasted "he had come there for the purpose of releasing them [the voyageurs] from their slavery."[18]

No sooner had Hervieux set up a tent on the beach east of the stockade than Simon McTavish and one of his numerous nephews, Duncan McGillivray, marched out and ordered him to move away from their men. Hervieux protested, showing his license, but the Nor' Westers retorted that it "amounted to nothing." When he didn't move fast enough, McGillivray returned "in a great rage" with a mob of cronies. As Hervieux later recalled, McGillivray "grasped his hunting knife and with it pierced the tent." One of his companions "then tore up the pins of the tent, which had fallen, and seized a bale of goods and threw it into the air. . . . He then advanced threateningly . . . saying, 'Sacré petit noir, if you were at Rat Portage you would see what I would do to you. . . . I would break your neck.'" When the marauding bourgeois found that one of their men had bought a tent from the intruder, they burned it as an example. Later, Hervieux's employers brought McGillivray to court in Montreal and won a settlement—but the company had proved its point. In 1805 voyageur contracts were changed to stipulate that any employee caught trafficking with "petty traders or Montreal men" would forfeit his wages.[19]

Profits were not the only issue in the Hervieux incident. The North West Company also felt keenly the necessity "to keep their engagés and men in submission." It was the era of the French Revolution. Old systems of authority were under question, and fear of mobs and rebellion was everywhere. By the 1790s the score or so bourgeois at Grand Portage looked out on 1,200 men camped around them and knew they were "beyond the aid of any legal power to enforce due obedience." From time to time rumors flew that the voyageurs were plotting attack. In 1794 panic raced among the bourgeois when "a few discontented persons" among the voyageurs en route to Rainy Lake began talking about "how much their Interest suffered by the passive obedience to the will of their masters." As Duncan McGillivray told it, these "rascals" inspired an entire brigade to demand "with one voice that unless their wages would be augmented, and several other conditions equally unreasonable granted them they would immediately sett off to Montreal." The strike, however, was soon quelled. In

*The Voyageur* by Abby
Fuller Abbe, about 1860

the end, there never were any major rebellions at Grand Portage—a fact the
company put down to "the good opinion these men entertain of their employers."[20]

## Building Up the Post

Surprisingly, there are almost no records of the development of the Grand
Portage depot. We do not know when the buildings were constructed or
who laid out the site. No pictures, plans, or complete inventories survive.
We have not a single post journal or the diary or letters of anyone in charge.
For Fort Charlotte, no eyewitness left even a single description.

The North West Company evidently took over the site, and possibly the buildings, of one of its ancestor companies of the 1770s. We do know that in the 1780s the company expanded its complex of buildings on the bay to house the valuable goods and furs that arrived each summer—£50,000 worth in 1784, and more every year that followed. Archaeology suggests that the depot was enlarged twice—first on the west and then on the north. By 1799 the company estimated that it had £25,000 of property at the portage, "a great risk and heavy Charge for any one Man." When it abandoned the depot in 1802, the value of the buildings was put at £30,000.[21]

The North West Company was never alone at Grand Portage. Independent fur traders camped there unnoted. Of more concern to the company was the periodic competition from Montreal—"the opposition." Since Grand Portage was a strategic bottleneck, anyone who controlled it could control trade to the northwest. The big company constantly tried to monopolize access to it. In 1787 the Nor' Westers petitioned the Quebec government for a grant of land encompassing the portage in exchange for improving the path into a wagon road. The request was denied, so the company resorted to fencing off tracts of land. In 1796 an American government official reported that the Canadian company had fenced "every Inch of Ground upon the portage . . . that might admit of buildings stores &ca under various and frivilous [sic] pretences." But this was an exaggeration. Three years later the company's manager at Grand Portage got a letter from his superiors in Montreal warning that the opposition would "try to build somewhere on the point, where the Montreal canoes usually pass the Summer, or about the premier's scaffold." He was instructed to take possession of these sites "by erecting a couple of Tents on the proper places & getting out the Montreal Canoes (that are remaining there from last Summer) on the point." The same year, the company plotted to buy up all the canoes on the Pigeon River side to force the opposition to run "the expense of sending Canoes across the Portage."[22]

As soon as the American Revolution was over, the North West Company petitioned for permission to establish a fleet of sailing ships to supply Grand Portage. The British government, which still maintained military dominance on the Great Lakes, was reluctant to ease controls on transportation, fearing "a clandestine illicit Commerce" by American traders poised to "debauch our friendly Indians." But lobbying by the company's Montreal agents gradually had an effect. In 1786 the North West Company launched the forty-ton *Athabasca,* and by 1790 it had two more ships of twelve and fifteen tons. These were inadequate, and in 1793 the seventy-five-ton sloop *Otter* was launched. Under Captain John Bennet, the *Otter* shuttled between Sault Ste. Marie and Grand Portage four times each summer, taking five to eighteen days each way. The main cargoes were food going west and hides returning, but the ship also carried building materials, livestock, and, doubtless, furniture for the post. By 1799 Grand Portage had two wharves and four boats to serve the *Otter,* which occasionally wintered and was repaired there.[23]

In the years when the ship's crew wintered at Grand Portage, the men joined a small year-round staff that maintained the buildings, looked after the animals, planted the gardens, and traded with the Indians. Only a few of their names are known. In 1785 the post was entrusted to Zacharie Cloutier, "a very respectable old man" of clerk-interpreter rank, assisted by a clerk named James Givens. He was later replaced by a higher-ranking *bourgeois,* though he stayed on at Grand Portage as an interpreter. In 1797 a partner named Simon Fraser was in charge. The next year he was replaced by Henry Munro, who served in the double capacity of post manager and doctor for two years. After that, Kenneth McKenzie took over. Five or six laborers also spent the winters, many of them going *en dérouine* to live with the Indians in their hunting camps on Lac des Chiens and Lac des Bois Blanc. Some of them were skilled workmen, such as a blacksmith and joiner. Although no record survives, most probably had families. At the typical fur post, women and children outnumbered the men.[24]

Two or three men were also stationed at Fort Charlotte. In 1793 a man named Donald Ross was said to have "been so long in charge of Fort Charlotte that he has acquired the respectable name of Governor." He was, however, replaced the next year by a clerk named Lemoine, "a Gentleman of a respectable [French] Canadian family." Lemoine's tenure was short, as he was charged with "some nasty tricks" and dismissed.[25]

The presence of year-round posts at each end of Grand Portage doubtless changed the lives of the local Ojibway. A fur post was a safe haven where the old and infirm often settled; it was a place for men to leave their families while out hunting or at war; and it was a source of income. Traders, on the other hand, needed Indians nearby to provide them with snowshoes, canoes, guides, information, furs, and food.

The Grand Portage Ojibway did bring in furs, but never very many—twenty packs in 1800 was a good return. The relationships revolving around food probably had much more impact on the band. Grand Portage was better supplied with food than many posts, for it had shipped-in stores of corn, biscuit, sugar, flour, and rum, besides its small herd of livestock and its potato gardens. But its residents still faced hunger in winter, for traders typically lacked both skills and equipment to supplement their diet from the land. In this predicament they depended on the local Indians to supply food. A post manager would hire one or two hunters and fishermen to provide food through the winter, and he would buy additional supplies from the local band.[26]

This was a familiar system to the Ojibway and Cree, who had age-old customs of sharing. Food was never hoarded, but freely given to anyone who had none. The Indians shared their surpluses with the post, and they expected the traders to reciprocate in times of famine. Most complied, realizing the necessity of conforming to social norms. So the post was integrated into the Indians' seasonal subsistence pattern as a kind of food bank. They borrowed food when they needed it and shared it when they didn't.

The post made it possible for the Grand Portage Ojibway to spend less time scattered in isolated winter hunting areas inland and more time congregated in the village on the lake. To support the winterers and themselves, they stepped up their wild ricing on the inland lakes in September, fishing on Lake Superior in November, and maple sugaring in March. In spring they sometimes invited their favorite traders to a celebratory *festin à tout manger*—a feast where all the food must be consumed. One who got such an invitation wrote that "each guest was served with a small bundle, neatly tied, of *orignal* [moose] dried meat of the best quality; but my appetite could not do justice to the whole of my *portion*. A friend close by me, observing my embarrassment, asked the rest saying 'I shall manage it for you.'"[27]

Food was not all the Indians provided. The traders were always in the market for canoes. The going price for one in the 1790s was about one hundred dollars. The large Montreal canoes were made in Trois Rivières and at St. Joseph on Lake Huron, but the twenty-five-foot North canoes were almost entirely of Ojibway make. In 1792 the Rainy Lake band was the main source, but the Grand Portage Ojibway also provided their share. In 1799 they had contracts for thirty-five canoes, of which the company expected twenty-five to thirty to be delivered. With the Indians constructing so many, it seems unlikely that the North West Company had much of a canoe yard at its depot, as it would later at Fort William.[28]

By the 1780s the local Ojibway included several regional groups. On the shores of Lake Superior were the Omushkasug. Farther inland lived the Bois Forts, or Sugwaundugahwininewug. Along the chain of waterways lived the Kojejewininewug, and south of them the Omushkegoes. The political center of all these divisions was at Rainy Lake, where the elders "meet in council to treat of peace or war" under the leadership of a well-known chief called Nectam, or the Premier. Nectam was a famous ally of the British. Years later, travelers mentioned the burial scaffold of a "distinguished chief" that was erected at Grand Portage and later moved to Fort William. As a mark of respect, the North West Company placed a British flag over the remains, an act that "was extremely gratifying to the Indians." It may be that Nectam was the chief so honored.[29]

The fur trade brought the Ojibway problems as well as opportunities. One was the influx of tribespeople from farther east, trying to make a living in the fur trade. Particularly unwelcome were Iroquois, itinerant trappers who "do not feel the same interest, as those who permanently reside here, in keeping the stock of animals good." Other people needed help. An Ottawa family was thrown upon the charity of the local Ojibway when both of its adult men died at Grand Portage. One of the children, an adopted white boy named John Tanner, later recalled: "As the weather became more and more cold, we removed from the [Grand Portage] trading house and set up our lodge in the woods that we might get wood easier. . . . Thus we lived for some time in a suffering and almost starving condition, when a Muskegoe, or Swamp Indian, called the Smoker, came to the trading house, and learning that we were very poor, invited us home with him to his own country, saying he could hunt for us. . . . He took us into his own lodge, and while we remained with him, we wanted for nothing. Such is still the custom of the Indians, remote from the whites. . . . [T]hose who were too young, or too weak to hunt for themselves, were sure to find some one to provide for them."[30]

By the late 1780s Grand Portage was beginning to have all the marks of permanence: a major complex of buildings, year-round employment, an Indian village. But this fur trade community was built on the shakiest of ground. It was, in fact, illegal.

## "A Dish of Grande Portage politicks"

Simon McTavish must have celebrated when peace broke out between England and its former colonies. His company had been dodging wars almost as long as he had been in the business. With peace, interest and insurance rates might go down. But any relief he felt turned to horror when news of the Peace of Paris reached Montreal in 1783. The English had agreed to a boundary line across the middle of the Great Lakes, leaving every major fur post—Niagara, Detroit, Michilimackinac, and, worst of all, Grand Portage—on the American side. "The idea overwhelmed our minds with the prospect of such certain ruin to the most valuable commerce of these provinces," a group of Canadian merchants wrote. Should the boundary go into effect, "the remaining Indian Trade of these Provinces would hardly be worth retaining or pursuing."[31]

The surrender of Grand Portage had been a mistake. The negotiators, looking at an incorrect map, thought the chain of border lakes was navigable to Lake Superior and had drawn the line straight through the lakes in order to give both countries equal access to the waterway. They did not know that the only route to the Pigeon River lay overland, five miles south of the border.[32]

As the shock wore off, the merchants took stock. The fur trade south of the Great Lakes was twice as large as that to the north, but an astute observer like McTavish could see that it was dwindling, while the northwest trade was just taking off. But "the Grand Portage is the Key to that part of British America." "It is indispensably necessary," McTavish and his cohorts told the government in 1792, "that the *Grand Portage* be thrown into our hands, or at any rate, that it be considered an open highway, equally belonging to both parties. . . . Without this, even the part of the North West still within our limits would become useless."[33]

If the traders were upset by the treaty, the Indians were outraged. They had fought on the British side because their interests coincided. The British knew that the fur trade depended upon the native work force and an undisturbed forest habitat. American settlers, on the other hand, wanted land. The British had formally acknowledged Indian title to the west and acted to prevent encroachment by the colonists. But the Peace of Paris, in which the Indians had no say, surrendered their territory to the land-hungry Americans. The high-handedness of this was recognized even at the time. "The Indians are free and independent people if ever any on earth were so," the Montreal merchants reminded their government. "*Our* running a Line of boundary by Treaty conveys no *right* of Territory without obtaining *one* from the aboriginal proprietors. We cannot give what is not our own."[34]

The issue stayed moot for many years. The new American government was far too busy to worry about the west. The British stayed in possession of their forts, still trading in territory that was nominally American. But the problem would come back to haunt both traders and Indians.

In the meantime, the North West Company had other worries. The annual meeting of 1784 was a disaster. The previous winter the Montreal partners had put their heads together and drawn up a new agreement that redistributed the company's shares so that many of the oldest traders were excluded or demoted. When this proposal was unveiled at Grand Portage, it met an explosion. Peter Pond stormed out. Two other snubbed winterers—Peter Pangman and John Ross—joined him and decided to form an opposition company. That winter they secured the backing of a Montreal firm called Gregory, McLeod and Company. Under its name, they prepared to challenge the Nor' Westers.[35]

The years had taken a toll on Pond. He was forty-five, an age when most men had retired from the rigors of the trader's life. But his ambition had not faded. In the isolation of the long Athabasca winters he had taken to brooding on the problem that had obsessed La Vérendrye years before: how to reach the western sea. Pond's years of travel had given him an unparalleled knowledge of western geography, and he had drawn a map to prove it. But like La Vérendrye, he was naive about the ways of bureaucracies. In the winter of 1784–85 he traveled to New York, then to Quebec, trying to interest the American and British governments in his discoveries and in a river route he thought would lead to the Pacific. The British thought his map "very curious," but neither government took action. Disillusioned, Pond gave up his resolve to form an opposition and rejoined his old friends at the North West Company. In 1785 he was back in Athabasca licking his wounds and growing ever more bitter and eccentric.[36]

Pond's defection did not stop Gregory, McLeod. In the spring of 1785 the new opposition sent four canoes to Grand Portage to challenge the North West Company's twenty-five. Along with those canoes went the most significant imports the company would make: two young cousins from the Scottish Hebrides, Alexander and Roderick Mackenzie.[37]

Alexander was twenty-one and already a *bourgeois*. Born three years after Alexander Henry's men first crossed the Grand Portage, he had spent a disrupted, Dickensian childhood: by age eleven he had lived in three countries and seen the last of both parents. At fifteen he entered "the count-

A portion of the 1785 map drawn by Peter Pond

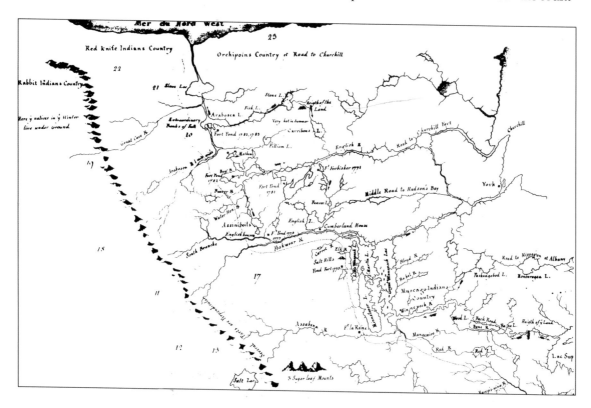

ing house of Mr Gregory" (as in Gregory, McLeod). There, his intelligence and initiative so impressed his employers that they made him a partner in the firm. He was perfect for a trader: "blond, strong and well built," with a "frame of body equal to the most arduous undertakings" and a confident flair that made men "ready to go with me wherever I choose to lead them." But his long, introspective letters reveal a more complex story: an intense, moody person prone to bouts of superhuman exertion followed by months of black depression, anxiety, "vain Speculations," and disturbing dreams.[38]

Roderick—or "Rory," as Alexander affectionately called him—was of a different cut. An "industrious, methodical man" who loved books and later tried vainly to write one, he seems to have gotten along with virtually everyone he ever met. He was assigned to spend his first winter at Grand Portage, clerking for Pierre L'Anniau, who was in charge of the opposition's fort.[39]

When Rory arrived at the portage he found that the new company's main winterers, Pangman and Ross, already had erected "one *hangard* or store warmly put together, and sufficiently spacious for the purpose of the season." Roderick's fellow clerks, who were "few in number and not of the first quality . . . did not seem to like doing the ordinary drudgery attending the general *rendez-vous* . . . so that I, who could yet claim no privilege, necessarily became the fag of the whole; but I did not grumble, though I often made the *comptoir* [counter] my pillow." After the outfits were off, Roderick settled down to the routine of Grand Portage life. The main job that winter was the erection of buildings, a job that employed eighteen voyageurs. It is not known where the buildings stood.[40]

Despite the competition, Roderick became "good friends" with the North West Company staff in the nearby depot. But relations with his own superior were less smooth. L'Anniau "had been for many years in that country, and was so handy that he was considered a 'jack of all trades,'" but he was illiterate and given to drink. "I made it my duty to keep a sharp eye over my gentleman," said the young Scot. After one binge he called the old man into the office, demanded the keys, and "assumed the charge and became master. This pleased all."

The genial Roderick quickly caught on to the techniques of the trade: "In the Fall, when the Indians were about the place, the young men and I became great friends, which, on their return with their hunt in the spring, they did not forget." When the company's partners arrived from the west, they found Roderick very much in charge and all but one of the local Indian families camped "within the limits of our Establishment."

The next year Roderick was deemed experienced enough to winter in the west, so he set out for English River under the command of his cousin.

William McGillivray

The Great Hall was re-
constructed in 1974 on
the basis of historical
research into the design
of the original building.

There he formed another fast friendship with an opposition clerk—a young nephew of Simon McTavish named William McGillivray, who was spending his third winter in the west. Roderick wrote that "in the Spring, after the trade was over, my neighbour and I, after comparing notes, agreed to travel in company to our respective head-quarters [at Ile-à-la-Crosse], where our canoes arrived side by side, the crews singing in concert." But not all business that winter had ended in such harmony.[41]

The canoes from Athabasca were late that summer. The two companies were already holding their separate rendezvous at Grand Portage when Rory McKenzie came hurrying in from English River with the news. John Ross, one of Gregory, McLeod's partners, had been killed in a confrontation with North West Company men. Once again, the evidence pointed to Peter Pond.[42]

The two companies met, probably in the North West Company's Great Hall. The Gregory, McLeod people were demoralized by "the direful effect the late opposition has had upon those that were engaged in it and upon the country." One of their partners was dead, another lamed, all felt their lives in jeopardy—and they were losing money to boot. Having beaten them down, Simon McTavish now made them an offer they couldn't refuse: the North West Company would increase its shares to twenty, and Gregory, McLeod's partners would get four. The opposition had little choice. It took

the bait, the partners consoling themselves that at least the Nor' Westers had been "compelled to allow us a share of the trade."[43]

The next question was what to do about Peter Pond. Someone had to go to Athabasca and keep an eye on the man. The person selected was young Alexander Mackenzie. It was a fortuitous choice.

That winter rumors about Pond flew among the fur posts. "I am quite surprised at the wild ideas Mr. Pond has of matters which Mr. Mackenzie told me were incomprehensibly extravagant," one *bourgeois* wrote. But Mackenzie wasn't laughing. Alone with Pond over the winter, he learned the old trader's theories, studied his map, and contracted the Northwest Passage fever. By February he was writing his cousin secretively about his "distant intentions," which "I beg you will not reveal . . . to any person, as it might be prejudicial to me." The next summer Pond had to go back east, possibly to clear himself of murder charges, and Mackenzie was left in command in Athabasca. Over the winter he laid his plans. In the summer of 1789 the partners at Grand Portage were surprised when Roderick instead of Alexander arrived with the Athabasca furs. They learned then that Alexander had set out to explore Pond's river of the west.[44]

The river was a disappointment. After an arduous, 1,500-mile journey, Mackenzie ended up standing on the shores of the Arctic Ocean watching beluga whales cavort amid the ice floes. Though he had "discovered" the Mackenzie River, it was not what he had been looking for. The next year he went back down to Grand Portage and found his cohorts unimpressed. McTavish's only reaction (in Mackenzie's exasperated words) was "a very severe letter . . . respecting the Athabasca packs of last year." The Marquis took the young *bourgeois* to task for having run off to explore rivers while leaving the furs "without a proper person to conduct them &c. &c. and desires in general that it must not be the case in the future and so forth." Mackenzie found "every thing quiet" at Grand Portage. "Every body had plenty of Letters and news from Montreal except myself. . . . My *Expedition* is hardly spoken of but this is what I expected."[45]

If Mackenzie was disappointed, Pond was destroyed. The map he had spent half a lifetime drawing was obviously incorrect. Bitterly he sold his share in the company to William McGillivray and left the west never to return. A sigh of relief must have gone up at Grand Portage.[46]

Mackenzie could not get the western sea out of his mind. He was torn. Increasingly interested in company politics, he itched "to mix in the business at the Portage" each summer, but another river beckoned. In 1793 he wrote his cousin, "I have been so vext and disturbed in mind since the beginning of this month that I cannot sit down to any thing steadyly. . . . I never was so undecided in my intentions as this year, regarding my going to the Portage or remaining in land." In the end, he opted for the west.

With a handful of voyageurs and two Indian guides, he set out up the Peace River. Traveling with astonishing speed, they dragged their canoes over the Rocky Mountains and descended to the Pacific coast, the first recorded group to cross North America.[47]

It was a year before Mackenzie could return to Grand Portage with the news. He spent the time in the grip of depression, tormented by dreams and visions of the dead. In January he wrote Rory, "What a pretty Situation I am in this winter. Starving and alone, without the power of doing myself or any body else any Service." He wished that "we could contrive matters so that we could both go to the Portage. MacTavish having come to Canada [from England] . . . we may expect him at the Portage, when it will be neceassry [sic] for every person concerned to meet." But when he arrived in that summer of 1794, McTavish was not there, Grand Portage was simmering with conflict, and Mackenzie was thrown into the midst of it all.[48]

The problem had been brewing a long time. In 1787 Benjamin Frobisher had died, leaving his brother Joseph in charge of the largest Montreal supply house in the business. Simon McTavish, knowing that "Joe" had never been much of a businessman, quickly wrote him: "Ever since the death of my worthy friend, your Brother, I have been considering in what manner our business in the N.W. can be best managed, so as to keep up our present influence and interest in that country." He pointed out that "your being alone, will render it impossible for you to attend to the business here and above," and noted his own dislike of "go[ing] every year to the Portage, which is unavoidable for any person largely interested in that country." He therefore proposed "to join our Fortunes and names in a general copartnership." Joseph readily agreed, and the firm of McTavish, Frobisher and Company was born.[49]

From the outset McTavish, Frobisher was a juggernaut. It owned almost half the shares of the North West Company outright and controlled others. Soon it was the company's sole Montreal agent. But McTavish did not stop there. To control the London end of the trade he and John Fraser (a family member) founded McTavish, Fraser and Company, which was soon marketing and exporting North West Company furs. McTavish was relentless in his pursuit of new markets. He shipped to China in competition with the East India Company. He recruited an up-and-coming businessman named John Jacob Astor to import North West Company furs to New York. The demand soared and so did profits. The company's yearly returns rose from about £30,000 in 1784–86 to £197,695 in 1803. "Every year brought with it enlarged operations and accession of capital," one observer wrote. Soon "the North-west Company [was] almost irresistible in Canada."[50]

All this was not accomplished without controversy. McTavish acquired "the reputation of a tyrannical and domineering leader." And yet he had a talent for co-opting rather than crushing the people and companies that opposed him. His invariable strategies were merger and acquisition—competition was to him a vulgarism. His pursuit of power was underlain by Old World attitudes. He loved to control through patriarchal benevolence and conspicuous noblesse oblige. Clannish as any Scot of Bannockburn, he shamelessly promoted his own family. He became fabulously rich but still hankered after the old marks of honor: a family crest, a landed estate, and, most of all, a title. In a rare fit of sentimentality, he bought the family estate in Scotland from the impoverished heirs when the chief of Clan Tavish died.[51]

The wintering partners of the North West Company well knew that the growth of McTavish, Frobisher was sapping away their power. There was an inbuilt conflict of interest between winterer and agent, a conflict intensified by cultural differences. Good eastern business practices did not always sit well with the experienced, self-reliant westerners. As McTavish worked for centralized control, the winterers had less and less input on the quality of goods and other decisions. The man they had regarded as their agent now seemed to view them as hired hands. They looked askance at the way the Marquis was packing the ranks with his own relatives. First it seemed as if there was a McGillivray under every stone. Then Frasers and McDonalds started sprouting up everywhere, as McTavish found jobs for second cousins and in-laws. And it was not lost on the winterers that the Montreal partners were building vast mansions while they starved in log huts.[52]

When the wintering partners arrived at Grand Portage in 1794 they found that McTavish had not come for the annual meeting, sending instead William McGillivray, the young nephew he had been grooming as an heir. Disgruntled by this snub, the partners gathered around a champion: Alexander Mackenzie. To Mackenzie, fresh from his winter of isolation and depression, such recognition must have been heady stuff.

So the stage was set for one of the classic confrontations of fur trade history, the decade-long battle of Mackenzie and McTavish, much of it played out in the Great Hall at Grand Portage. It was more than just a clash of personalities. On one level, Mackenzie represented men who had made the fur trade a way of life. McTavish represented those for whom it was a way of making money.

The discontent of 1794 came to a focus in a stormy meeting the next year when Mackenzie spearheaded an effort to renegotiate the North West Company's agreement. He succeeded in wresting several concessions for the winterers: McTavish actually ceded some shares for the sake of peace, and he accepted limits on his power to make decisions without a majority vote from the partners at Grand Portage.[53]

The Marquis's reaction was typical. Seeing that Mackenzie had become the lightning rod for a rift in the company, McTavish quickly acted to co-opt him. He offered the younger man a partnership in the inner sanctum of McTavish, Frobisher. Dazzled, Mackenzie accepted. When he next arrived at Grand Portage, he was McTavish's representative.[54]

But McTavish soon found that he had not neutralized Mackenzie, who remained a champion of the men in the field. Mackenzie's philosophy was that capital could be raised anywhere, any time, but good employees were made only by experience. He saw the company as "an association of men of wealth to direct, with men of enterprise to act, in one common interest" but structured so that "the latter may succeed the former, in continual and progressive succession." The company needed more room at the top for the "men of enterprise" like himself.[55]

Alexander Mackenzie

Mackenzie also acted as a cultural broker for the winterers. An anecdote illustrates his intermediary role. The winterer Jean Baptiste Cadotte (the half-Ojibway son of the man who had started Alexander Henry in the trade) had gotten deeply in debt to his father's old partner. Cadotte, who had had an eastern education and a handsome inheritance, was a good trader but a poor money manager because his cultural values of "open-handedness and generosity to his Indian relatives" always left him impoverished. Unknown to Cadotte, Henry prevailed on Mackenzie to buy the winterer's debt at a discount. One summer at Grand Portage Cadotte interpreted for Mackenzie during a difficult council with the local Ojibway. Afterwards Mackenzie walked him to his canoe, shook his hand, and gave him a sealed paper. On the way to his post Cadotte opened the paper and found a "clear quittance of all his indebtedness to Alexander Henry, which had always been a trouble on his mind. . . . [H]e ordered his canoe turned about, in order that he might go and express his gratitude to the generous McKenzie [sic], but on second thought he proceeded on his journey, imbued with a firm determination to repay this mark of kindness by attending closely to his business." With such stories circulating, it was no wonder the winterers looked upon Mackenzie as an ally. Later, the voyageurs would nickname him "Le Chevalier," gilding him with the aura of the old French nobility.[56]

For a while it seems Mackenzie (who had scarcely known his own family) tried to fit into the close-knit McTavish clan. He and William McGillivray outwardly got along like brothers—they shared rooms and held competitive drinking matches that left their guests gasping. But under the surface there was also an unmistakable sibling rivalry between them. Mackenzie must have known that, no matter how heroically he worked, McGillivray would win any battle before it started, as long as Uncle Simon McTavish was around. Mackenzie would never be in the inner circle of McTavish's confidence; he was not truly one of the clan. The evidence is sketchy, but it seems Mackenzie secretly began to lay a daring plan:

no less than to oust McTavish from his own company. To do it, he would need the support of the winterers.[57]

In 1799 Mackenzie and McGillivray traveled together to Grand Portage, McGillivray little suspecting that his companion might be plotting a coup d'etat. Of the meeting that followed there are half a dozen accounts, all biased. Roderick, caught painfully in the middle, said Mackenzie announced to the assembled partners that he felt "uncomfortable" about "some misunderstanding existing between him and his Montreal associates . . . and was determined to withdraw from the Concern." This brought on "a very violent discussion between the wintering partners on the one hand and the agents on the other." The winterers declared that Mackenzie, "having their sole confidence, they could not dispense with his services, therefore . . . every means should be adopted to retain him"—apparently including the increased powers he was after. Duncan McGillivray, in a more jaundiced account of the "vexatious proceedings at G. Portage," accused Mackenzie of having made his dramatic announcement "in terms evidently calculated to inflame"; after passions were raised, "very unwarrantable measures were adopted to retain him. . . . In short many causes concurred to produce violence & disagreement for a little time." McTavish described it later as "a Dish of Grande Portage politicks."[58]

Simon McTavish

Fortified by the demonstration in his favor, Alexander Mackenzie returned to Montreal. What happened there no one knows. Apparently there was a confrontation in which Mackenzie made "unreasonable & inadmissible" demands. McTavish, enraged at finding himself the target, turned the tables, called Mackenzie's bluff, and reorganized McTavish, Frobisher to leave him out. The would-be ouster was ousted. After "a great deal of havering & irresolution," Mackenzie impulsively set out for England. William McGillivray, consummate diplomat, put a calm face on it all: "I believe finding at last he had carried matters too far—he would have preferr'd things were otherwise,—tho' we parted not on the best terms, nothing has past [sic] to prevent an amicable settlement . . . —hard indeed! would it be on us all, *on me particularly*, if after our long intimacy, we could only look on each other as Enemies in future."[59]

That winter John Fraser, McTavish's London partner, kept an eye on Mackenzie. Though he believed the young man had acted "entirely from a fit of ill-humour, without any fix'd plan or knowing himself what he would be at," he warned McTavish not "to fly off, as you seem to think you now have a right to do." Mackenzie still had power. "You know him to be vindictive, he has got an intire ascendant over your young Men, & if driven to desperation he may take steps ruinous to you. He has told myself Your Nt.West business will be completely ruin'd; to others he has thrown out most violent threats of revenge."[60]

It took two years for Mackenzie's revenge to take shape. But when it did it rocked the northwest.

## The Knight's Vendetta

McTavish brooded about the events at Grand Portage in 1799. In a letter the next spring he reproached the wintering partners: "I feel hurt at the distrust and want of confidence that appeared throughout all your deliberations last season, and particularly at the attempt which was made to dictate to my House in the appointment of its agents at the portage, which interference on your part is not warranted by our contract with you." But many of the partners had already had second thoughts, and support for Mackenzie was waning. In the end, as one witness put it, "not one of them joined the standard of the Knight."[61]

Though Mackenzie had failed to lead a revolution within the company, there were threats from outside as well. The Nor' Westers had not been alone at Grand Portage all these years. The competition consisted of a plethora of small companies, many of which also had interests south of the Great Lakes. The most noteworthy were the two Montreal firms of Forsyth, Richardson and Company (backed by the London firm of Phyn, Inglis and Company); and Parker, Gerrard and Ogilvy. McTavish's way of dealing with these firms had been to allow them a nominal share in the North West Company in return for a pledge of noncompetition. But this arrangement began to fall apart in the mid-1790s. The Americans were getting restless about continued British operations in the land ceded after the Revolution and had sent John Jay to negotiate a way to oust them. Signed in 1794, Jay's Treaty once more declared the territory south of the Great Lakes off limits. The companies operating there turned with new interest to the northwest. By 1799 McTavish was concerned. "The threatened opposition have, this year, made a serious attack to us, and I fear that a coalition of interests between the parties opposed to us may render them more formidable." In the end, however, he dismissed the impact of what "the new adventurers to the North-West may clip from our wings."[62]

The coalition he feared took place that year. The new opposition was called by several names—the New North West Company was popular, but the one that stuck was the XY Company, allegedly from the marks on their bales. Still the Nor' Westers were not concerned. "It is said they must fail for want of *Capital*," wrote one.[63]

But there was a source of capital waiting to be tapped. Alexander Mackenzie had made a fortune in his years at McTavish, Frobisher. Since his move to London he had become quite the celebrity in England's high society. He published a book about his explorations, hobnobbed with royalty, and in 1802 was knighted by George III. It must have galled the title-conscious McTavish to hear the words "Sir Alexander Mackenzie."[64]

And Mackenzie was still simmering. Only the year before he had scoffed at the "pityfull . . . appearance" of the XY Company, but by 1800 he was ready to sign on. He wrote a friend that joining the competition against "those for whom I had . . . the Sincerest regard" would "be one of the severest trials to my Feellings, but McTavish & his relatives Treatment of me is such that I may for a time forget I had Friends & even forget . . . my Interests." In short, he knew he could make no money in the opposition. He could only have revenge.[65]

In 1802 the XY Company officially became Sir Alexander Mackenzie and Company. That year Mackenzie was back at Grand Portage, organizing the rendezvous. The firm already had some buildings there. In 1799 a man named L'Etang, working for Forsyth, Richardson, had gotten "a Hangard and House erected by Men at a Dollar per day." These were probably the structures an 1802 visitor found "a few hundred yards to the East of the N.W. Co below the hill." But Mackenzie thought them inadequate and soon had his men building "a very fine 'fort' upon the hill." By 1803 the work was finished. "Situated on the brow of a sloping hill, over a mile from the landing," the new fort had a view that was described as "very fine." The perimeter was marked by "palisades of tall cedar pickets with bastions at the four corners. Within the enclosure were several good buildings for the use of members of the Company, and towering over all was an immense flagstaff from which, on Sundays and when heralding the arrival of the principal bourgeois, floated a large and very handsome flag." This impressive structure may have stood on the present site of the Catholic church or the school. From an 1803 inventory we know it contained at least twenty-three panel doors, thirty window sashes, ten bedsteads, twenty-four chairs, and three japanned candlesticks.[66]

The new company also erected a complex of buildings on the Pigeon River end of the Grand Portage, across Snow Creek from Fort Charlotte. On the Lake Superior side it had a barn and animals. In 1803 Mackenzie was able to travel to Grand Portage on the company's new eighty-five-ton schooner, the *Perseverance*, under Captain White—a harrowing, storm-tossed journey that nearly brought the company to an untimely end.[67]

The Nor' Westers were agog at the amount of capital the XY people were investing. "The sacrifices they have made to procure Men are incredible," said Duncan McGillivray, who had replaced Mackenzie as agent for McTavish, Frobisher. "They throw away their means with a profusion that astonishes the Men themselves." Traders in the field felt the results. One, faced with an XY Company rival, said, "For eleven years that I have been wintering among the Savages I have never known a competitor trade as cheaply as Chorette. I think Lucifer brings him his goods from London as he needs them." The XY Company was willing to lose money. It was not a business. It was a vendetta.[68]

Throughout his life, Simon McTavish's reaction to a challenge had been compromise and accommodation. Not this time. If the "Little Company" (as he scornfully called it) wanted war, so be it. McTavish wanted nothing more than to crush Mackenzie, and he could play hardball.[69]

Events at Grand Portage prefigured what would soon be happening across the west. In 1802 XY clerk George Nelson found Grand Portage in a stew of lawlessness. One of his company's brigades bound for the west camped with its goods on the Pigeon River near Fort Charlotte, "where they feasted & got drunk upon the 'régale' that was always given them when they arrived from, or departed for, their winter quarters. When they arose the next morning they found thirty Kegs of High Wines . . . had all run out! Upon examination it was found they had been bored with two gimlets holes each! . . . These were called *witty tricks*. Rumor gave out that it was Benjamin Frobisher [son of Joseph] who bored the Kegs. It created an excessive bad feeling & led to retaliations some of which would have ended tragically but for providence."[70]

Another incident soon followed. Nelson was about to set out for an XY post in Wisconsin with three *engagés* whose contracts with the old company had expired. As they were loading the canoes, Duncan McGillivray came down to berate the men for changing allegiance:

> *A quarrel ensued. We were at dinner. The men came running up saying Mr McGillivray was going to carry off the men by main force. 'The Knight' [Mackenzie] ran down, we all followed. And no small affair it was, all in words, menaces & gestures indeed, but those are often the fore-runners of blood. We at last embarked fully determined to defend ourselves, fight, & kill, if driven too it; & armed for the purpose. Mr McGillivray got into a boat with a couple of men, he hailed their vessel that was then anchored in the bay,—the Captain sent out the Jolly boat, But they at last gave up the chace, assuring us however, that they would come upon us at night; and for several days we were in great fear.[71]*

Though Nelson saw no bloodshed, others did—"in the 'North,' it was 'neck or nothing.' *They* did not 'stickle at trifles.'" On the Saskatchewan, a clerk named James King was killed by an opposition counterpart. On the Assiniboine, Daniel Harmon heard more rumors of bloodshed and worried that "most of us soon should have cut one anothers throats." A shocked Hudson's Bay Company trader claimed that "the Country all over is in a ferment of murder and robbery so that men were not in safety to stir out."[72]

The traders did not confine their aggression to each other. In fact, the Indians suffered most. Normally, competition was advantageous to them, for they could—and did—drive down prices by playing traders off against one another. But without many of the social controls that had existed before the smallpox, traders' tactics got more violent. Theft, beatings, and harassment were not uncommon. On the Red River, Alexander Henry the Younger (nephew of the old trader) recorded how he assaulted a party of women in order to steal furs the XY Company had already paid for, though he claimed to be "vexed" at "the necessity of fighting with the women." It vexed him less to steal a horse and administer a "cruel beating" to a man who hunted for the opposition. "I . . . stopped up his Eyes, so that he could not see for several days," Henry wrote with evident satisfaction.[73]

Grand Portage was not immune. John Tanner's Indian family, which was taking 120 beaver skins east to sell, found that passing over the portage was like running a gauntlet:

> When we reached the small house at the other side of the Grand Portage to Lake Superior, the people belonging to the traders urged us to put our packs in the wagons and have them carried across. But the old woman [Netnokwa, Tanner's adoptive mother] knowing if they were once in the hands of the traders it would be difficult, if not impossible, for her to get them again, refused to comply with this request. It took us several days to carry all our packs across, as the old woman would not suffer them to be carried in the trader's road. Notwithstanding all this caution, when we came to this side the portage, Mr. McGilveray [Duncan McGillivray?] and Mr. Shabboyea [Charles Chaboillez?], by treating her with much attention, and giving her some wine, induced her to place all her packs in a room, which they gave her to occupy. At first, they endeavoured, by friendly solicitation, to induce her to sell her furs; but finding she was determined not to part with them, they threatened her; and at length, a young man, the son of Mr. Shabboyea, attempted to take them by force; but the old man interfered, and ordering his son to desist, reproved him for his violence.

In the end, however, all the pressure paid off. The traders got the furs by manipulating Netnokwa's son, and the family was left destitute.[74]

But the traders knew that strong-arm tactics were not enough, for they only alienated the Indians and encouraged them to drop out of the trade relationship. Somehow traders had to find an incentive for the Indians to hunt more, to push into new lands. The Indians' limited desire for material goods made them too independent. Traders needed a controlling lever. Alcohol and tobacco were their solution.

Alcohol had always been part of the fur trade. Normally it was not sold, but given as a diplomatic gift or as part of the food-exchange system. Its use had been kept down partly by its symbolic role, for the Indians normally drank only as a function of ceremonial situations like trade or funerals.

Alcohol was also kept scarce by the difficulties of transporting it, government regulations, and traders' distaste for dealing with the crime and disruption it caused.[75]

But a trade war could not be won through business as usual. Like no other commodity, alcohol could buy goodwill and even, because of its symbolic overtones, pseudokinship ties. Supplied in large enough quantities, it could also become physically addictive; then there would be no need to worry about sales resistance, since demand would always go up. Duncan McGillivray reasoned with the devastating logic of a drug dealer: "When a nation become addicted to drinking, it affords a strong presumption that they will soon become excellent hunters." And that was all the traders needed.[76]

In the years before the XY Company was formed, the North West Company had shipped an average of 9,600 gallons of liquor into the west each year. By 1803 the total had shot up to 16,299 gallons, and the opposition was bringing in 5,000 more.[77]

Indian society was unprepared for the onslaught. At the time it had few rules or taboos surrounding liquor. The resulting violence and social dysfunction were mainly turned inward, ghettoized in Indian villages, only rarely breaking out. Even so, longtime traders with Indian families were shocked and sickened. But Duncan McGillivray and policymakers like him blamed the "wretched Indians" and the competitors who had "compelled" the North West Company to set the west awash in rum.[78]

As Indian hunters struggled to meet traders' demands for food and furs, exploitation began to exhaust the delicately balanced forest habitat. Food became scarce, and tribes were forced to compete for territory. Confrontations erupted, often egged on by traders who wanted "their" Indians to expand hunting lands through war. The situation was to no one's long-term advantage, but very profitable to a few people in the short term. Ethnohistorian Harold Hickerson perhaps put it best: "Rampant spoliation meant immediate enrichment of major traders and Company, but exhaustive impoverishment for the Indians and the minor figures of trade."[79]

Meanwhile, Simon McTavish was building himself a castle three stories tall, of dressed limestone, bastioned by circular towers with conical tops and covered with a high peaked roof. It stood on a plateau looking down on Montreal, a city now "torn with factions" allied with himself or Mackenzie. As the elderly Alexander Henry remarked, "There could not be two Caesars in Rome." Even old friendships fell. Roderick McKenzie had married the sister of McTavish's wife and taken a job in McTavish, Frobisher, leading to a break with Alexander. When the cousins resumed correspondence years later, they addressed each other frostily as "Dear Sir."[80]

In both 1801 and 1802 McTavish was back at Grand Portage, suspicious even of his allies. To discipline his wayward partners he pushed through a program of austerity. Any partner found abusing alcohol—a companion risk to the increased liquor trade—would be expelled. Any partner who engaged in competitive trade would be fined £5,000 for each share he held. No longer would the company supply wintering partners with more than their "personal necessaries"—later explicitly defined to limit status symbols like light canoes, excess baggage, and more than one servant. In a new company agreement McTavish wrested significant powers from his partners, including authority to "hire and employ all Clerks, Interpreters and *engagés*."[81]

Then, in 1804, with the west bubbling in rum and mayhem, Montreal at odds, and his mansion half finished, Simon McTavish abruptly died. He was fifty-four years old.

His heir apparent, William McGillivray, quickly stepped into his place. His first act was to do what McTavish himself would have done in saner times—he offered the olive branch to Alexander Mackenzie. In fall the two companies met and negotiated a merger. The North West Company inherited mainly debts, and the XY Company got a quarter of the shares in the reorganized firm. But it was a Pyrrhic victory for Mackenzie. The one stipulation McGillivray would not negotiate was that "Sir Alexander Mackenzie is excluded from any interference" in the company.[82]

The news traveled like wildfire across the west: the war was over. The next summer the two companies would meet together at a single rendezvous. But it would not be at Grand Portage. Other events had overtaken the old site of so many conflicts. The North West Company would henceforth have a new headquarters and a new route to the west.

## Leaving the Post

It was a problem with boundaries that led to Grand Portage's downfall. Back in 1796, the "fatal moment" the traders had feared so long had arrived: by the terms of Jay's Treaty, the British had to vacate their posts south of the border. But that year came and passed, and the North West Company was still at Grand Portage. Rumors flew the next year: the Americans were coming to build a military post at the portage. No, the customs collector at Michilimackinac was coming to charge duties on all the goods that passed through. Later they heard that "United States troops had actually landed at Michilimackinac . . . for the purpose of proceeding to the depot of the fur trade, at the Great Carrying-place, and there enforcing the duties." The company was beside itself. Alexander Mackenzie and two Indians surveyed the north side of the Pigeon River to see if there was a way through, but they found nothing but "high falls, rapids, and shelving precipices."

There seemed to be no alternative.[83]

As the partners were mulling their boundary problems, a new employee arrived at Grand Portage. He was no ordinary recruit. David Thompson was a Welshman who had been educated at a London charity school and at age fourteen assigned to the Hudson's Bay Company, which sent him into the wilds of Canada. Trained as a surveyor, he had spent the next thirteen years traveling thousands of miles for the English company. Later, he would discover the sources of the Columbia and other routes to the Pacific. But he was scarcely the romantic figure his accomplishments call to mind. Meticulous and puritanical, he was the sort of man who, once told a rule, followed it till he died. To one observer he was "a singular-looking person . . . plainly dressed, quiet, and observant. His figure was short and compact, and his black hair was worn long all round, and cut square, as if by one stroke of the shears, just above the eyebrows. . . . [H]e has a very powerful mind, and a singular faculty of picture-making. He can create a wilderness and people it . . . so clearly and palpably, that only shut your eyes and you hear the crack of the rifle, or feel the snow-flakes melt on your cheeks as he talks."[84]

In 1797 Thompson decided to jump ship to the North West Company. When he arrived at Grand Portage in July, he was just the man the partners needed. No one knew where the boundary ran. Half of the company's posts might be on the American side. In the next year Thompson, who was listed as the Grand Portage post astronomer, traveled in a four-thousand-mile circle around his home base. He first went west, locating the boundary as far as Lake of the Woods, then to the northernmost curve of the Missouri River, since it might be considered part of the Mississippi in some future treaty. He then traveled back through northern Minnesota, locating the region of the Mississippi headwaters, then around the south shore of Lake Superior. At Sault Ste. Marie in spring, he met Alexander Mackenzie on his way to Grand Portage, who told him that "I had performed more in ten months than he expected could be done in two years."[85]

But Thompson's survey had not eased the partners' minds on the central issue—what to do about Grand Portage. It was the Indians who finally came to their rescue. As Roderick McKenzie was traveling from Grand Portage to Rainy Lake that spring, he overheard some local Indians talking about another way to Lake Superior. When he asked, they pointed out the old route by the Kaministikwia River that the French had used. "This was excellent information," he said. "Of course I immediately engaged one of the Indians to . . . show me this new route." Even he admitted that "it is most astonishing that the North-West Company were not acquainted with it sooner."[86]

It was not a perfect solution. The men complained that the new water route was made up of "brooks rather than Rivers." The canoes had to be loaded more lightly for the shallow water, and the distance was longer, so that "the *voyageurs* had to be coaxed and bribed into the use of it." But the route had one enormous advantage: it ran north of the border. Simon McTavish, who had never had much sentimental attachment to Grand Portage, immediately ordered that "no time should be lost in moving our place of *rendez-vous*."[87]

By 1800 the company had men at work draining the "dead Swampy flat" at the mouth of the Kaministikwia, where the new depot would stand. It was to be a structure grand enough to put the XY Company to shame. By one account the move cost the partners £10,000 and would have cost more but for the fact that they wrested "a certain number of days of forced labour" from each canoeman, which "cost them little." The rendezvous of 1802 was the last the North West Company held at Grand Portage. The next summer the new depot was still unfinished, though Alexander Henry the Younger found "great improvements had been made here for the space of one Winter season, Fort, Store, Shop, &c built, but not a sufficient number of dwelling houses for all hands. . . . We were under the necessity of erecting our Tents for our dwelling. . . . Building was going forward very briskly in every corner of the Fort, and Brick kilns were also erected and turning out great numbers, so that we shall have every thing compleat and in good order before our arrival here next year." In a few years, the sprawling new complex was christened Fort William in honor of William McGillivray, the now-unchallenged ruler of the North West Company.[88]

The local Ojibway tried to dissuade the company from moving. All this fiction of boundaries within their land had an ominous ring. "They claimed the country as their own," wrote William Warren, the half-Ojibway son of a trader, "and felt as though they had a right to locate their traders wherever they pleased." Moreover, they would not "acknowledge the

Sketch of Fort William by Robert Irvine, 1812

right which Great Britain and the United States assumed, in dividing between them the lands which had been left to them [the Indians] by their ancestors, and of which they held actual possession."[89]

Despite these arguments, the traces of Grand Portage's long fur trade oc-
cupation were fast disappearing. On leaving, the North West Company
"destroyed their forts and warehouses." The scarcity of building fragments
found by later archaeologists suggests that many structures were dis-
mantled and shipped up the coast to the new site. The XY Company held
its rendezvous alone until the merger in 1804, when it too abandoned its
brand new depot on the hill. For a few years the North West Company
kept "a clerk there with two or three men, as a mere Indian trading post."
But by 1822, when David Thompson returned, once more surveying the
boundary—this time for the government—he found that "scarce a vestige
remains of all the former Factories; they are covered with rank Grass, and
in places a little fine red Clover."[90]

The North West Company, which in its years at Grand Portage had
commercialized the continent from Lake Superior to the Pacific, walked
away with scarcely a look back.

# CHAPTER FIVE

# Roots of Community

Traders, who thought of themselves as the central figures of the frontier, rarely realized how unimportant their existence was to the Indian community. When the North West Company abandoned Grand Portage, the local band's world did not collapse. Ojibway life went on as usual.

In the early nineteenth century about 150 Ojibway people lived in the Grand Portage region, between Grand Marais and Fort William. They were organized into several groups, possibly divided by clan. On the south were those led by a chief named Espagnol, who often camped around Grand Marais. To the north was the band of Peau de Chat, who could often be found around Fort William and Whitefish Lake. Other loosely organized

*Grand Portage* by Eastman Johnson, 1857. The view was painted looking east from the site of the old depot toward Mount Josephine.

groups led by men like Shaganasheence and Grand Coquin used land in between. Grand Portage was a popular summer camping ground for all of them, though only fifty or so seem to have spent the majority of their time south of the border.[1]

Their small number reflects the harsh and depleted land where they lived. Ever since the 1760s travelers had been reporting that the Grand Portage region was "very destitute of all sorts of game." By 1824 a trader at Fort William wrote that moose and deer were "literally extinct. Caribou was also at a former period, and not a great many years since, very numerous. Few now are seen—the scarcity of these Animals is greatly felt by the Indians. In Winter their sole dependance for Subsistance is on Rabbits & Partridges." Five years later another Fort William trader complained that even the scant 195 who did business there were "by far too many for the district."[2]

And yet they survived, using time-tested strategies for coping with scarcity. Their relationship to the land had to be one of deep and detailed knowledge: they knew each good fishing hole, each deer yard and path, each berry patch and stand of birch. The place names they used reflected their knowledge: for example, Wauswaugoning Bay (The Bay Where They Spear Fish by Torchlight) and the Mawskiquawcawnawsebi (High Bush Cranberry Marsh River, the present Reservation River). They knew the habits and life cycles of a myriad of animals and plants. Because any one resource might fail, they always depended on a variety. Their ethic of sharing ensured that all would have enough but no one would have a consistent surplus.[3]

They moved frequently and far in order to balance the resources of the inland with those of the coast. Fish was their staple food, and the fishery was the center of social life. Unlike the Lake Superior of today, the waters then teemed with three types of trout (weighing from five to fifty pounds each), sturgeon, pickerel, pike, black bass, herring, whitefish, and crayfish. The women wove nets up to 360 feet long of nettle-stalk fiber or manufactured line, the meshes carefully measured to catch particular species, the floats of wood, and the sinkers of stone or lead. When a species began its run to shallow spawning waters—usually in late summer or fall—the men set the nets in huge semicircles from canoes. Women preserved the catch by smoking the fish or by hanging it up by the tails to dry.[4]

As winter set in, the people broke up into smaller hunting bands and moved inland to the shelter of the forest surrounding the smaller lakes, particularly Whitefish and Arrow. Winter fishing depended on a good coat of ice. Some families carefully threaded their nets under it with a long pole. Others either set baited lines or lured the fish into spearing range with a carved wooden fish on a string. If the fish gave out, the people would move on to family hunting territories. Hunting lands were passed down from father to son.[5]

When the sap began to run in March, the families often split up, the men going on a spring hunt and the women, children, and old people to the sugar bush. In those days, a stand of maple trees stretched parallel to Lake Superior from the Pigeon River to Maple Hill north of Grand Marais. One favorite sugaring camp lay between present Reservation and Trout lakes, and a well-known trail connected it to Grand Portage Bay. Just as hunting lands were partitioned among the men, so the women had use rights in certain sections of sugar bush. They tapped the trees, boiled the sap down in huge brass and copper kettles, granulated it with paddles in a wooden trough, then pressed the sugar into carved molds. After sugaring season they left all the tools in the woods with no fear that anyone would disturb them.[6]

Some summers were spent in the sugar camp, but more often the band gathered at Grand Portage Bay. There people might spearfish by torchlight on Wauswaugoning Bay, set lines or dip fish in the Pigeon River, or make an occasional hunting trip to Isle Royale. By early autumn wild rice was ripe on the inland lakes—particularly Whitefish, Gunflint, and Northern Light—and families crossed the portage to harvest it and to hunt migratory birds in the rice beds. Not everyone in the band made each move; people were constantly splitting off, joining new groups, and trading foods.[7]

Despite their intricate adaptations to the existing environment, the Indians also altered the land in their favor. Their most important tool was fire. Deer prefer young forests with undergrowth, elk like prairie clearings, and moose, caribou, and game birds use open bogland. To provide for a diversity of species, the Ojibway set fires, creating a marbled forest where stands of young and old trees coexisted. In the *grand-brulés* (as the voyageurs called the burnt-over tracts), gooseberries, raspberries, and blackberries throve—attracting bears as well as people. As burned areas regenerated, young aspen sprang up and provided food for beaver, which built dams that kept water tables high for wetland species. Over time, the Ojibway could create productive habitats for wildlife and themselves.[8]

The temporary summer village at Grand Portage was the focus of ceremonial, political, and (on rare occasions) military activities. This was not a hierarchical society like that of the fur traders. The community at large made important decisions in council, through long discussions. The leadership tended to change with the situation. There were civil chiefs (often a hereditary position), war chiefs (usually achieved), clan chiefs, religious leaders, and the "headmen" of the smaller hunting bands. One person might hold several roles, but no one had the absolute authority of a European ruler. Leaders functioned by personal prestige and persuasion. As a French observer put it, an Ojibway chief "can not say to them: 'Do this and so,' but merely—'it would be better to do so and so.'" An Englishman agreed—"All the force of their government consists in persuasion."[9]

We have only scraps of information about the Grand Portage band's leaders. During the 1820s a trader reported that "there is one principal chief to whom the others in great measure look up—the only name he goes by, even with the Indians, is 'Espagnol.'" Said to be descended from a Spaniard on his father's side, Espagnol was "no less celebrated from

*Ojibwe Women* by Eastman Johnson

*Wigemar Wasung,* Johnson's charcoal and crayon sketch of a Lake Superior Ojibway woman

shrewdness of intellect as for valuable hunts." At an 1841 council he was described as "a tall and handsome man, somewhat advanced in years . . . arrayed in a scarlet coat with gold epaulettes . . . with the air of a prince." Since he hunted in American territory, the traders at Fort William felt that Espagnol "must be more liberally treated than any other of our Indians." Accordingly, they plied him with generous gifts, grumbling behind his back that he was "the most troublesome Indian ever I met with." In the harsh winter of 1837–38, when he was fifty-four, he became *windigo*—a kind of demonic possession, very difficult to cure, whose sufferers were said to crave human flesh. The next summer he converted to Catholicism at Grand Portage and took the name François. Later, he moved across the border.[10]

The Peau de Chat family, related to Espagnol by marriage, was also prominent at Grand Portage in the 1820s. The original Peau de Chat was an elderly man then, but he had at least three sons and a brother, Grand Coquin, who was also considered a chief. By 1850 their band had moved north and Joseph, one of Peau de Chat's sons, had assumed leadership of

*Kenne waw be mint.*
Johnson sketched resi-
dents of Grand Portage
and other north shore
communities during
1856 and 1857.

the Fort William Ojibway. A missionary the previous year described Joseph as "a man of about 40, tall and well built, with a vibrant, sonorous voice. His eloquent enthusiasm and vehement impetuosity have caused the Indians to elect him as their chief."[11]

Shaganasheence, whose name meant "Little Englishman," was born at Rainy Lake but was head of a hunting band at Grand Portage by the 1820s. John J. Bigsby, a British traveler whom he guided along the boundary in 1822, recalled him as "an active young Indian." He was, said Bigsby, "a most useful fellow. Like the rest of his tribe he wore his hair long, and plaited into twenty or thirty slender strings, which were weighted with bits of white metal interwoven at regular distances. As some of these hung over his face . . . when he wanted a clear sight he somehow, in an instant, shook them all behind him." Later Shaganasheence became a Catholic and took the name Joseph. In the 1850s he represented his band in treaty negotiations with the United States.[12]

The Caribou clan has always been prominent in the Grand Portage band, and its leader through the mid-1800s was Addikonse, or Little Caribou. Those who met him described him as "statesman-like," with a "genuine dignity of mein [sic] and manner." Born about 1789, he claimed never to have touched liquor and eventually became an ardent Catholic. Well-known for his oratory in treaty negotiations, he earned a reputation for "good character, wisdom, integrity and inflexible firmness."[13]

Besides such leaders there was another kind of chief—the "fur chief" created by traders. Ever since Europeans and Indians first met, the flexibility of Indian leadership traditions had frustrated the whites. Often they had tried to impose a more formal system, and by the nineteenth century they had the power to make it stick. The traders chose men with whom they could work (or whom they could manipulate) and loaded them with gifts, uniforms, and other symbols of power. Later, government agents followed suit. Bands were forced to deal with non-Indian powers through these appointees, whom they had not chosen and for whom they often had little respect. The hereditary and clan chiefs, seeing their power undermined, protested. "You wish to snatch away my power and give it to another," Joseph Peau de Chat told British authorities in 1849. "You intend to make a dissolute savage chief of the Band. I tell you that you are usurping our authority. Neither the queen nor the chief in Montreal can ever alter what the Indians have enacted." Despite such protests, the pattern would be repeated.[14]

For a few brief years after the North West Company left, it seemed as if the tide of history might be turning in the Indians' favor. Changes began with a religious revival that reached Grand Portage about 1808. Messengers from the east brought the teachings of a man called the Shawnee Prophet. Much of his doctrine involved rejection of European ways and goods such as flints and steels: "The fire must never be suffered to go out in your lodge. Summer and winter, day and night . . . the life in your body, and the fire in your lodge, are the same. . . . You must never strike either a man, a woman, a child, or a dog. . . . From this time forward, we are neither to be drunk, to steal, to lie, or to go against our enemies."[15]

The Shawnee Prophet's religion "spread like wild-fire." At the Ojibway village of La Pointe on Madeline Island, the shores of Lake Superior were strewn with medicine bags cast into the water as the prophet required. "Drunkenness was much less frequent than formerly, war was less thought of, and the entire aspect of affairs among them was somewhat changed by the influence of one man," wrote one eyewitness.[16]

The religious groundswell soon became a political and military movement. The prophet's brother, Tecumseh, advocated tribal solidarity against invading settlers. Soon, war broke out in the Ohio River valley between the U.S. Army and Tecumseh's confederacy. In 1812 Britain joined its Indian allies in the war, in hopes of recapturing trade and territory lost in the American Revolution.

Recruiters soon appeared at Grand Portage. In 1812 the Americans heard that one of the Cadotte family and John Askin, Jr., were "collecting all the principal Chiefs" from Grand Portage, Fond du Lac, and Mackinac for a council of war. Later, trader Robert Dickson came to Fort William loaded down with medals, flags, and promises, ready to recruit Ojibway warriors. Some joined, but after two wars many had become disillusioned. "When I go war against my enemies, I do not call on the whites to join my warriors," one Pillager Ojibway said. "The white people have quarrelled among themselves, and I do not wish to meddle in their quarrels."[17]

They had good reason for skepticism. The Shawnee Prophet's promises of invulnerability in war proved cruelly wrong. Even Tecumseh was struck down in the Battle of the Thames in 1813. The religious excitement died away. Former believers "hung their heads in shame," and the name of the prophet was despised. But no better were the promises of the British. Though the Indians captured Mackinac, Detroit, and other key fur posts on the Great Lakes, the British gave them all back across the treaty table in Ghent. Indians, traders, and soldiers alike were outraged at the diplomatic betrayal. "Our negociators, as usual, have been egregiously duped," one British commander wrote bitterly.[18]

The Treaty of Ghent in 1815 set up a process for resolving the knotty problem of the boundary west of Lake Superior. The British, seeing a chance to capture back the Grand Portage, claimed everything north of the St. Louis River. The Americans responded by demanding everything south of the Kaministikwia. The dispute lasted till 1842, when both sides finally settled on the Pigeon River line but designated the Grand Portage a free passageway for both nations—which it remains today. In the meantime, the Ojibway grew used to seeing boundary surveyors. In 1822, when David Thompson passed through on a British survey team, a local chief asked him: "What is your purpose in rambling over our waters, and putting them into your books?" Thompson explained as best he could and added that "the Indians would not be disturbed in any way."[19]

Nothing could have been further from the truth.

## End of a Company

Up to 1821, despite occasional contacts with warring governments, the Grand Portage band's main link to the outside world was still the North West Company, which clung tenaciously to its trade south of the border. When an American-licensed trader named De Lorme tried to pass over the Grand Portage in 1806, the traders at Fort William dispatched a crew to harass him. They "proceeded to fell trees across the road, at the portages, and on all the narrow creeks" to teach the upstart a lesson. Border or no border, the company also maintained a small seasonal post at Grand Portage and occasionally wintered its schooner at the mouth of the Pigeon.[20]

Times were changing for the North West Company. Always as much a subculture as a business, it had now become something more—a community. Two generations of mixed-blood children had grown up since the British first came west. By the 1790s, priests were shaking their heads at the size of the unbaptized mixed-blood population at Grand Portage. By 1806 the North West Company decided that the families of its men were becoming a "heavy burthen to the Concern" and instituted a penalty for marriage to an Indian woman, since "a sufficient number, of a mixed blood, can be found." Nevertheless, by the 1820s the number of traders' dependents in the west had grown to 1,200 or 1,500. Around each major fur post sprang up a little community of retired voyageurs, women, and children. Many of the mixed-bloods—or *métis,* as they sometimes called themselves—entered the fur trade. Others chose to join their Indian relatives, who "cherished [them] as their own." But as the population grew, both tribes and company reached the limits of their ability to feed new mouths.[21]

The company itself had become top-heavy with personnel. The organization was perfectly adapted to expansion—but by 1805 the continent had been spanned and the company was up against the hard reality of finite resources. In 1804 one of the partners had worried that "the hunt is declining very fast, and we are obliged every year to make new discoveries and settle new posts. . . . I believe that our discoveries are now about at an end, and that the trade cannot be extended much farther." By 1812 the Hudson's Bay Company foresaw its rival's doom: "I am afraid their ambition and enterprize have carried them too far." The North West Company either had to adapt to the stable conditions of a permanent trade or perish.[22]

The company did not die quietly. Its expanding operations had placed it cheek by jowl with its old competitor, the Hudson's Bay Company. That old fossil of feudalism had itself been undergoing changes. After 1807 a majority of its stock had fallen into the hands of an obstinate, idealistic young Scotsman—Thomas Douglas, earl of Selkirk. From his commanding position, Selkirk devised a series of humanitarian schemes aimed at aiding Scottish peasants dispossessed as a result of British industrialization. One such scheme was an agricultural colony on the Red River near the present site of Winnipeg, in the heart of North West Company territory.

Settlement had always been anathema to fur traders, and this one was no exception. A series of confrontations led to armed war between traders and colonists. In 1816 Selkirk set out for the Red River through the Great Lakes with a group of Swiss mercenaries to put the feisty Nor' Westers in their place. At Sault Ste. Marie news reached the earl of the bloodiest conflict yet: twenty-one colonists lay dead at Seven Oaks. In a rage he swooped

Thomas Douglas, earl of Selkirk

Small room in the Great Hall at Fort William, 1816. This sketch is said to have been drawn by Selkirk while he and his soldiers occupied the fort.

down upon Fort William, had his soldiers seize the fort, and threw the astonished William McGillivray and his deputies into the brig.

During the winter that Selkirk and his mercenaries occupied Fort William, he turned some attention to the old Grand Portage. He moved at least one building there from Fort William and grazed some of his many cattle on the ruins of the North West Company's headquarters. He also set his soldiers to cutting a thirty-six-mile road between Fort William and the Pigeon River. Where it ran is unclear; some said the southern terminus was at Fort Charlotte, others chose Goose Lake (perhaps today's North Fowl Lake). The remains of some cedar log bridges were still visible in the late 1800s.[23]

The conflict had weakened both companies. Selkirk's untimely death from tuberculosis opened the way for reconciliation. In 1821 William McGillivray once again led his partners into a merger—but this time it was the North West Company that was absorbed, and McGillivray met the same fate he had once served to Alexander Mackenzie. "I part with my *old troops* to meet them no more in discussion on the Indian trade," he wrote during his last visit to Fort William. "This parting I confess does not cause me much regret. I have worked hard & honestly for them. . . . We had too many storms to weather from without and some *derangement of the household* but, thank God! the whole is done with honor."[24]

Those who had no fortunes to retire on could not console themselves with thoughts of honor. With the merger, the Hudson's Bay Company abandoned the Great Lakes shipping route in favor of the cheaper sea route through Hudson Bay. Hundreds of clerks and voyageurs became unemployed overnight, and the provisioning and canoe-building industries that had supported the north shore Indian bands collapsed. Like Grand Portage before it, Fort William became a backwater post and soon started falling into decay.

In the 1820s the fur trade made a strained transition into a modern business. It was a bottom-line, acquisitive sort of era, with little time for the niceties of tolerance. George Simpson, governor of the Hudson's Bay Company's Northern Department, looked on the Indians not as partners but as laborers: "However repugnant it may be to our feelings, I am convinced they must be ruled with a rod of iron, to bring, and to keep them in a proper state of subordination," he wrote in 1822. Once freed from competition, the company began to cut back on diplomatic gifts, reduce the quality of its goods, and evict Indian families who had settled at the posts. Food, which had usually been exchanged as a gift, became a commodity to be purchased with labor. In the view of William Warren, a trader's mixed-blood son, "The Indian ceased to find that true kindness, sympathy, charity, and respect for his sacred beliefs and rites, which he had always experienced from his French traders." In the minds of the British, the Indians had become no more than "the hunting-slaves of a company of whites in Leadenhall Street."[25]

The traders could get away with such attitudes because of a shift in food relations. As *métis* labor became available, the posts—Fort William included—had developed agriculture and fisheries to an extent that made them nearly independent of Indian hunters. At the same time, game was so depleted that the Indians came more often to the posts during scarce times. The former reciprocal relationship began to lean toward Indian dependence. In July 1827 the traders at Fort William reported fifty Ojibway people living at the post, some laboring in the potato fields in return for food. By the next January the count had grown to seventy-two, and the larders were strained. "They have been always accustomed to be maintained at the Establishment during this month and next," the proprietor had explained to his cost-conscious superiors. "It is found impossible to refuse support . . . without great hazard of displeasing them and perhaps of losing them altogether."[26]

But the Grand Portage band had a bargaining chip for dealing with the Hudson's Bay Company. It was created by the boundary. To the south, where the British could not legally trade, the remnants of the North West Company's old Fond du Lac Department were now in the hands of John Jacob Astor's American Fur Company. The change in ownership meant little at the bottom, where the employees were mostly second- and third-generation traders connected to the Ojibway by marriage or blood. In charge of Fond du Lac (at present-day Duluth) was an experienced trader named William Morrison. The North West Company had no sooner ceased to be than Morrison was laying plans to move in on the British. In 1822 Ramsay Crooks, the American Fur Company's general manager, wrote that "Morrison will establish some new posts along our northwestern border. The old Grand Portage is allowed to be within our line, and there the N. W. have always had a good little post, since they retired to Fort William. An outfit from the Fond du Lac department should be sent to that place under some active men; and in order to keep our opponents on their own side of the boundary, our clerks or traders are to be made customhouse officers."[27]

The "active men" they sent in 1823 were a sullen clerk named Bela Chapman and several malcontent voyageurs. On the advice of the Indians, Chapman built his post at Grand Marais, a spot he glumly called "Fort Misery." He was ill-suited to winning over the Indians, whom he believed to "cheat lie and steal, the Devil is not a match for them. . . . [I]t is a pity such Indians should have a trader. . . . [M]ay they never return." Not surprisingly, he did little business. His presence was, however, of great use to the local Ojibway, who instantly reported the news to Fort William. The Hudson's Bay Company cut its prices and sent men to winter with the band "in order to prevent them from going towards the Americans." Espagnol expertly played the rivals off against one another. Chapman observed that "the Indians are not two well pleased with them [the Hudson's Bay Company] for all their low prices and fair promises[.] [T]hey say high time now they have an opposition." At the same time, the chief assured the British company of his loyalty: "They are very partial to us and say that if we would establish a post at the Grand Marrais, we would be sure of the best part of their hunts." In spring, Chapman made a trip to Grand Portage to get Espagnol's furs, but failed: "I have tried the force of flatery & of Lying & of Rum and he has withstood all." The Grand Portage Indians were putting their money on the English.[28]

The story was the same the next year, when John Johnston, half-Ojibway son of a longtime Sault Ste. Marie trader, made the trip to trade at Grand Portage and found that "persons in the service of the Hudson Bay Company carried off in trains [dogsleds] the band of Chippeways." By 1831 the border was the site of such "a constant, strenuous and desperate opposition" that a U.S. Indian agent recommended a military fort at Grand Portage to protect the "lives and property of our citizens." But the competition was quashed like others before it—not in the marketplace, but in smoke-filled rooms. In 1833 the two fur companies came to a secret—and highly illegal— agreement: American Fur would withdraw from the border in return for a payment of £300 a year from the Hudson's Bay Company. The only ones to suffer were the Indian customers.[29]

The Americans, however, still had plans for Grand Portage. The pact with the Hudson's Bay Company prevented them from trading furs, but it said nothing about fish. In 1834 John Jacob Astor withdrew from the fur trade, and a new American Fur Company was organized with Ramsay Crooks as president. Crooks quickly moved to diversify the Lake Superior trade. In 1836 he sent William A. Aitken, Morrison's successor in the Fond du Lac Department, to find sites on the north shore for commercial fisheries. Grand Portage and Isle Royale were the main locations Aitken chose. By the fall of 1836 American Fur had a crew of coopers and boatmen at Grand Portage under the direction of Pierre Coté, a mixed-blood from Fond du Lac.[30]

The Grand Portage fishing station operated much like a fur post. The American Fur Company provided the nets, barrels, and salt; the Indians provided much of the labor and know-how. From August to November they set nets where trout and whitefish congregated along the coast from Grand Marais to Pigeon River. Indian women cleaned the fish and salted them down in barrels, which Coté then purchased for three dollars apiece. The twenty Indians employed produced three hundred to five hundred barrels a year, which were picked up by the company's schooner, the *John Jacob Astor,* to be shipped east. An even larger operation on Isle Royale produced as much as two thousand barrels.[31]

Grand Portage had again become a bustling establishment by 1839. A visitor that year said there was "One dwelling House for Coté, situated on a gentle rising ground, overlooking the Bay, a dwelling occupied by his son on the West side, and a new Store fronting this last building on the East Side, forming a hollow square; Two mens houses, 1 Coopers Shop, 1 Fish Store, Stable Barn, Root house &c below or near the beach, placed here and there without order or symetry. . . . The dwelling houses and Store on the hill are finished in a Substantial manner and all new." There was also "an appology for a Store house" on Grand Portage Island and a three-acre field of potatoes that produced 200 to 250 bushels a year.

The Hudson's Bay Company looked askance at all this activity employing its erstwhile hunters. Though Crooks had carefully obtained their consent, the men at Fort William were astonished at the scale of the operation. In 1837 about a hundred Indian men with their families were fishing at Isle Royale. Even the traders at Lake Nipigon worried that "the establishment of the old Grand Portage by the American Fur Company . . . will cause many from this place to wish to pay them a visit next summer." And they suspected that that "spiteful wasp" Pierre Coté was not above trading furs on the side.[32]

The boom lasted only five years. The fisheries proved so productive that American Fur was soon buried under a glut of salt fillets. At the same time the panic of 1837 ruined the market for specialty foods. Desperately the company tried to get rid of the fish in New York, the Ohio River valley, and as far away as Texas, with no success. By 1841 Crooks had cooled on fish: "We are not inclined to prosecute the business with our former energy," he wrote. The next year his company failed, and the fisheries were never reorganized.[33]

## The Path of Souls

The year-round presence of the Coté family brought a new element to life at Grand Portage: Christianity. Pierre and his Ojibway wife, Margareth, were devout Catholics who aroused their neighbors' interest by reading from a prayer book translated into Ojibway by Lake Superior's most famous missionary, Father Frederic Baraga. By 1837 they had created such curiosity and hope about Catholicism that the chief of Grand Portage requested a missionary. That fall, Baraga himself arrived for a short visit from his headquarters on the south shore. The next year he sent a Slovenian priest, Father Francis Xavier Pierz, to establish a mission church.[34]

Father Francis
Xavier Pierz

It was not that the Ojibway lacked a religion. Ojibway life was so infused with religion that there was scarcely an act without a spiritual component. To them, the natural world was permeated by the sacred. One could not hunt an animal without first reaching an agreement with its spirit, or gather an herb without leaving an offering to the earth in return. One could not travel a stream without its permission. Natural events had meaning for those who could read them: the robins called for rain, meteors foretold sickness, and the owl was a harbinger of death. "We respect everything," said one Ojibway holy man. "We believe in the God, the *Manitou*, but we also believe in trees."[35]

For the Ojibway, ignoring the sacred was perilous. Acts like naming a child or singing a song could invoke grave powers. People paid strict attention to dreams, in which they glimpsed a world more real in some ways than the waking one. At puberty children fasted to seek a vision of their animal spirit guardian. "Without such a vision," wrote a modern Ojibway author, "a person was considered a child for life. And life had no meaning." The guardian protected and guided the person through life. There were many dangers—not only from temptations to err, but from ill-wishing *manitous* and men. "You couldn't laugh at a Indian years ago, or poke fun at him, because they were so powerful," said one Ojibway.[36]

There were many overlapping religious practices and organizations at Grand Portage. A prophet, or *jessakid*, could communicate with the spirit world through the shaking tent ceremony. There was a mysterious association called the *Wabenowin,* whose members studied the sky and revered the spirit of the morning star. Best known was the *Midéwiwin,* which Indian agent Henry Rowe Schoolcraft called a "grand national society devoted to the mystical arts." It was a medical fraternity and an organized priest-hood in one. Members of the *Midéwiwin* were also the guardians of tribal history, myth, and tradition, inscribed on birch-bark scrolls. Membership in the society was limited, and initiation was achieved after years of in-struction and payment. There were degrees of membership, each with its own secrets and techniques. The *Midéwiwin* met at Grand Portage in July for eight-day ceremonies.[37]

Despite these ancient beliefs, the social strains created by disease, war, and the fur trade left many Ojibway searching for new answers. The Shawnee Prophet's revival had proved illusory, but the hopes it had aroused still lay under the surface.[38]

Then, just before the new priest arrived, a miracle happened. A man who had been suffering from a seemingly fatal disease despairingly cast out the charms and medicine bags from his home, whereupon he recovered. When Father Pierz's boat arrived the cured man "walked into the water un-til it reached his waist, in order to be the first to shake my hand. All the rest, too, gave me a hearty reception."

There seems to have been an atmosphere of religious excitement that first year. The Cotés supervised the erection of a large cedar-bark chapel on the spot where *Midéwiwin* ceremonies had always been held. Pierz soon bap-tized sixty-four people ranging from five days to seventy-five years old. The high point was the baptism and wedding of the chief, Espagnol, which took place "with all [the] formality of the church service. He presented himself for this holy performance in a white coat trimmed in yellow, his loins girded with a beautiful red girdle, with red trousers stitched in white and with yellow shoes. I decorated him with a rosary and hung a beauti-ful cross around his neck after the custom of all the Catholic Christians in Indian country. His seventy-year-old bride appeared in a black dress . . . covered with white embroidery from head to foot and sprinkled with bright colored glass beads."

To most missionaries of the nineteenth century, faith was inseparable from culture—to be Christian, one must live as a Euro-American. Like the Shawnee Prophet before him, Pierz set out to change the Ojibway life-style, this time to include agriculture. He distributed tools and seeds, and the band enthusiastically cleared land along the Pigeon River for vegetable gardens and fruit trees. To inculcate European language and literacy, Pierz started a school that was attended by fifty-eight Ojibway and seventeen "French" (*métis* or French Canadian) students. "Here I preached to them ev-ery morning and evening," he wrote, "and held school for them the rest of the day, which every one under fifty faithfully attended. I taught four different groups in turn every day, reading, singing and religion."

For a year all went well. But in 1839 church politics resulted in Pierz's unwilling transfer to Michigan. Three years later he was able to return for a summer, at which time he moved the mission to the cleared farmland along the Pigeon River. There the Ojibway built him a new birch-bark chapel lined with cedar mats, big enough to hold a congregation of seventy. Pierz reestablished the mission school and revived his farm. He introduced cows, pigs, hens, and grain and taught the band the use of the sickle, scythe, plow, and hoe. But after he left that fall, Grand Portage was to see only brief missionary visits until 1848.

In that year three Jesuits arrived to revive Pierz's mission on the Pigeon River. What they found was a discouraging sight. "Here and there, a few unfinished houses, then, on a height of land in the centre, near the river bank, a wooden church which formerly lacked only a roof, but which now falls piece by piece; a little farther along was a house—if you would like a one-roomed cabin which lets in the light of heaven through the openings in the roof. That is the house we are to occupy." The Jesuits stuck it out for a year, but in 1849 the mission burned to the ground and the priests moved north to Fort William.

In 1854, and for twenty-three years thereafter, it fell to Father Dominique du Ranquet to commute by dogsled and canoe from Fort William to minister to the Grand Portage band. At first he used a bark chapel in the village. Then, in 1865 a new log church was consecrated to Our Lady of the Holy Rosary. Though covered with siding and paneled inside, that chapel still stands on the hill back of the reconstructed fur post, the principal church of the Grand Portage Reservation.

There are times in history when events seem poised to go several ways. For Grand Portage, as for much of the Minnesota region, the 1840s were such a time. A unique sort of community had sprung up in the wake of the fur trade: a multilingual, multiracial frontier polyglot reflecting each wave of culture—Indian, French, and British—that the land had appropriated to itself. Such communities operated by their own values and rules, sometimes developed their own distinctive art styles, and were linked all across the west by a webwork of kinship, commerce, and shared history. If left to develop another forty years, communities like Grand Portage might have reached a cohesion and identity that would have resulted in a far different cultural and political voice for the west in the years that followed. But events were to carry Grand Portage into a different future.

# CHAPTER SIX

# The Boundary of Cultures

Ages ago, an Ojibway prophet predicted that whites "would come in numbers like sand on the lake shore." It would be an "ending of the world." By the 1840s, it was clear that time was coming. Looking at the fates of tribes to the east, the Ojibway began to wonder if they were, as many whites insisted, "a doomed race."[1]

On the south shore of Lake Superior, deposits of copper and iron had been discovered, and developers were flooding in. As early as 1840 some leading men from Grand Portage told a fur trader that they dared not leave "their own land which they believe will soon be demanded by the U.S. Government, and . . . which they are afraid that others who have no right might dispose of without their consent." Soon those demands came. In 1849 a portion of the northern Ojibway traveled to Sault Ste. Marie to negotiate the cession of the entire Canadian north shore for £2,000 and yearly payments of £500. A Fort William missionary was bitter at the bargain: "Witness our poor Indians about to receive—not a fortune so great that they need never work again, as some fondly imagine—but some feeble aid which at least will help them buy clothing."[2]

In 1854 it was the turn of the bands south of the border. Representatives went to La Pointe, the ancient center of Ojibway settlement. Addikonse, the leader of the Caribou band, was determined not to suffer the fate of his northern relatives—he was "the last to yield title to their lands." He "long stood, *solitary and alone*, pitting himself, nobly, against the Government orators, and insisting that the proffers of annuities, &c., were inadequate." In the end the Ojibway won payments worth $19,000 a year for twenty years, plus a one-time bonus of goods in exchange for lands from Duluth to Rainy Lake. Each reservation got a blacksmith, and Grand Portage alone received a school. Unlike less hard-bargaining tribes, the Ojibway got reservations in the heart of land they already occupied. Four leaders signed for Grand Portage: Shaganasheence, first chief; Addikonse, second chief; and two headmen, Waywegewam and Maymushkowaush.[3]

With the signing of the treaty, the band's relationship with the United States changed. Legally, band members became wards of the federal government, which promised to act as their protector and advocate. Culturally, they became targets of a government project aimed at wiping out Indian identity and assimilating the Ojibway into the life-style and beliefs of Euro-Americans.

## Grand Portage Reservation

Only a core of the band members actually lived on the reservation—at first called the Pigeon River Reservation; the rest stayed in scattered settlements at Beaver Bay, Grand Marais, Red Sucker Bay, Lake Saganaga, Rove Lake, Moose Lake, Gunflint Lake, and elsewhere. Each major settlement on Lake Superior was dominated by a different clan: the Bear clan at Beaver Bay, the Caribou clan at Grand Marais, and the Crane and Caribou at Grand Portage. The reservation, which was later estimated to contain 51,840 acres, was administered by annual visits from the agent at La Pointe, across the lake.[4]

In the first few years after the treaty, the continuity must have been more striking than the change. The government hired Henry Elliott and Nelson Drouillard, who were already working at Grand Portage as traders. On a rise of ground east of Grand Portage Creek they erected a squared-log warehouse for storing annuities. A new sort of rendezvous began to happen each summer, as the scattered members of the Grand Portage and Nett Lake (Bois Fort) bands came to collect the promised payments. It was a festive event. One seaman who witnessed the payment in 1865 said that about 1,400 people were camped at Grand Portage when the boat arrived. "They had a good time of it, our cargo of supplies being divided among them."[5]

The school opened in 1856 when an "industrious and untiring" Irish couple, Timothy and Mary Hegney, arrived to serve as teachers. They taught forty-one children and twenty adults the first year, though less than half that number attended at any one time. "I have no great difficulty in keeping them under reasonable control," Timothy Hegney said, but he complained about absenteeism during sugaring and fishing seasons. By the end of the year, the best students could "speak a little English, tell the names of all objects familiar to them, and understand what they are told in English well." Though the teachers changed and sometimes there were as few as six pupils, the school remained open. In later years, it was the only government presence at Grand Portage.[6]

The government's main goal was to encourage the band to "adopt the habits of civilized men." To this end Drouillard, the blacksmith, supervised the clearing and cultivation of land and the building of "comfortable houses." Each Indian who lived in a house was rewarded with a cookstove, utensils, a table, bureau, chairs, bedstead, and a looking glass. In 1856, in a burst of enthusiasm, the government even surveyed a village plat at Grand Portage, laying out town lots, streets, and alleys. By 1860 the Indians were raising as much as three thousand bushels of potatoes a year, and it could be said that the reservation was in a "prosperous condition."[7]

In the 1870s the annuity payments ran out, and so did the cheerful reports. The agent showed his frustration: "It is a sad feature of my work, that I am not able to meet all the demands made upon me for teachers, farmers, &c. . . . I have no funds, my hands are tied." As for Grand Portage, "It has been impossible to find any kind of labor for them to do, even though we had funds to do it with." Concerned about alcoholism and violence, the Office of Indian Affairs sponsored an Indian police force and appointed three respected old men as judges—an unsuccessful attempt to replace tribal forms of government with Euro-American ones.[8]

Contacts with the outside world were becoming more frequent. At first, the newcomers to Grand Portage were still a familiar type: traders. From

Grand Portage schoolchildren with their teacher, John A. McFarland, in 1889

1849 to 1863, Hugh H. McCullough had a large trading business all along the border lakes: Saganaga, Basswood, Rainy, and Lake of the Woods, with an anchor post at Grand Portage. He employed thirty-six "packers"—probably local people—to haul supplies over the portages. On the Grand Portage he used ox teams. McCullough supplemented the trading business with commercial fishing between Grand Portage and Isle Royale.[9]

The first nontraders to arrive on the north shore were Yankee prospectors, trappers, fishermen, land cruisers, and a few settlers. Among the latter were Asa A. and Caroline L. Parker and their family, who in 1868 settled on the old Catholic mission site at Pigeon River, calling the place Parkerville. "We had a nice home, large home, as it seems to me now," their daughter Mary later recalled, "and several log buildings that were used by the Indian families who worked for my Father. The Winters were very severe and we were practically isolated. . . . [A]bout once a month the mail would arrive on dog sleighs or toboggans from Fort William." Mary recalled that once, when several of the family were laid low by scarlet fever, "my Oldest Brother (Aldis) might have died if the little old Indian woman 'Nokomis' [Grandmother] we called her had not taken such good care of him. When he got better . . . she would strap him on her back and tramp out to her traps and keep him in the sun shine all day." The Parkers themselves raised a local Indian boy, Henry Le Sage.[10]

For a short time Parkerville was a busy adjunct to the Grand Portage community. To Parker's trading post the Indians brought their furs in winter and spring, maple sugar in spring (made up in "wee canoes" of birch bark for the children), and berries ("by the water pail full") in summer. Years later, local residents still remembered the Parkers' gardens full of potatoes, vegetables, and flowers: lilacs, pansies, even English violets. The family left in 1874, but the townsite would be inhabited again.

The panic of 1857, followed by the Civil War, slowed immigration to the region, but in the 1870s it picked up again. The height was in the 1890s, when booming fisheries lured migrants from Norway, Sweden, and Finland.

The immigrants brought a new attitude—to them, land needed to be used, changed, and developed. In that brash, expansive era, resources existed to be stripped away, and the culture's heroes were entrepreneurs who made quick fortunes and moved on. The difference between the newcomers and the Indians was the difference between tapping a maple tree over many years and cutting it down for a quick profit.

The main resources of the north shore, minerals and timber, took only thirty years—1880 to 1910—to strip away. Thirty years of prosperity were followed by decades of impoverishment.

Even before the treaty of 1854 was signed, Superior, Wisconsin, was crowded with mineral prospectors poised to find fortunes in the newly opened land. One of them said, "What conversations I heard around me all turned toward copper claims. There were rumors of great masses of pure copper and large veins . . . that could be traced for long distances." On the Canadian side, mining companies had been at work since the late 1840s, and one of them was prospecting at the mouth of the Pigeon. Indian men soon found jobs guiding eager mineral seekers, hauling supplies, staking claims, and digging the test pits that still dot the countryside. Hopes soared in 1868, when a fabulously rich silver mine was discovered at Silver Islet on the east side of Thunder Bay. In 1884 visions of riches came even closer when Oliver Daunais discovered a vein of silver on Whitefish Lake, where the Grand Portage band once wintered. The mine, called Silver Mountain, soon made a boom town of the Canadian settlement of Port Arthur, near Fort William. A railroad was built to carry the ore to the docks at Port Arthur, and a whole complex of mines sprang up, with names like Beaver, Badger, Porcupine, Crown Point, and Rabbit Mountain. The Whitefish Lake mining region employed so many men from Grand Portage between 1885 and 1911 that a well-worn trail connected the two spots. But on the United States side all hopes were dashed. Despite an attempt to mine copper on Susie Island, no significant mineral deposits were ever found on the American side of the north shore.[11]

Timber prospectors followed hard on the heels of the miners. Today, when the forest attracts droves of nature lovers, it is hard to realize that most early non-Indian settlers looked on it with fear and hatred—as a dark refuge of savage animals, supposedly bloodthirsty Indians, and forest fires. In 1900 a Grand Marais high school graduation speaker hopefully described a day when "all that vast forest has gone and in its place is a large and noisy city." It looked like she might get her way. Around 1893, Alger, Smith and Company, which had already logged huge tracts in Ontario, Wisconsin, and Michigan, bought up several hundred million board feet of pine north of the Pigeon River, adjacent to the reservation. In the summer of 1898 the company established a base camp a quarter-mile from the river's mouth. Like fur trade depots before it, the camp complex included a warehouse, office, stables, blacksmith shop, harness shop, cookshack, bunkhouse, and dwellings.[12]

That winter the cutting began. It was a huge operation. The logs were hauled on skids to the Pigeon River and its tributary lakes. With the thaw in spring, the river-drive crews took over. Floating the logs down the zigzag chasms on the Pigeon would have reduced them to toothpicks, so the Pigeon River Improvement Slide and Boom Company built $48,000 worth of elaborate wooden sluices, dams, roads, and aqueducts to carry the logs safely to the lake. In Pigeon Bay, booms gathered the logs into enor-

Logging dam at the beginning of Split Rock Canyon on the Pigeon River, shown here in 1922. When the dam was closed, water was diverted through a sluice that bypassed the cascades and two river bends.

mous rafts to be towed to the Alger, Smith sawmill at Duluth, said to be the largest one on the continent at that time. The 1899 raft contained ten million board feet of lumber.

In 1900 a second firm—the Pigeon River Lumber Company—joined Alger, Smith, building another base camp at the river's mouth. For a few years Pigeon Bay was a busy harbor served by shuttling steamers. But at such a rate, it did not take long to strip the land. After only four years, Alger, Smith sold its stumpage, sluices, and camps to Pigeon River Lumber and left. By 1919 that company, too, pulled out, leaving the countryside bare and the people jobless.

For a short time the mineral and lumber bonanzas benefited the Ojibway. The men found seasonal employment, and the sale of reservation timber, which the government encouraged, brought income. In 1889 the band agreed that reservation land not owned by individual Indians be logged off, but the government apparently did not proceed with the timber sale until the first decade of the twentieth century. Between 1907 and 1911 A. V. Johnson of Grand Marais cut about 3.7 million board feet of pine. Cutting of cedar, spruce, and other trees used for pulpwood continued on and off till 1929, when they too gave out.[13]

In the long run, the logging had less desirable effects. The cutover acreage was prone to terrifying fires, some of which threatened even the village on the bay. The marbled forest ecosystem was reduced to a uniform second growth, robbing residents of many hunting and trapping resources they had relied on. And white entrepreneurs' eagerness to acquire Indian timber led to frauds that bilked many Indians out of their land.

A third resource—fish—took longer to deplete. It survived till the 1950s, when the predatory sea lamprey, introduced into Lake Superior by increased water traffic, almost wiped out the native fish. But in the 1880s and 1890s, itinerant Scandinavian fishermen regularly cruised up and down the north shore, taking herring, trout, and whitefish. In 1889 band members complained to the government that these fishermen, some of whom camped on Susie and the other islands just outside Wauswaugoning Bay, spread nets so large that they monopolized the fish. Around the turn of the century a more permanent fishing station started up at Grand Portage, this time on the island. It was the business of a French Canadian named Pete Gagnon, who worked with A. Booth and Company of Duluth. Gagnon had a store, a house, an icehouse, two dwellings for his hired fishermen, and a long dock for visiting steamers. In addition he opened a general store, rented rooms to visitors, and ferried goods and people to the mainland. He

Nanette Gagnon, Bessie Gagnon Plante, Frank Paro, Sr., and Pete Gagnon photographed by Frances Densmore on Grand Portage Island, 1905 twice married women from the Grand Portage band—Nanette May-mushkowaush and Lucy Spruce.[14]

In 1882 a government harbor project at Grand Marais offered jobs, and so many Ojibway moved there that they formed an eastern suburb called Chippewa City. In 1895 they got their own Catholic church, St. Francis Xavier, a hewed-log structure that still stands, though the community around it was largely wiped out by the influenza epidemic of 1918. Relations with their neighbors seem to have been quite cordial. In the 1890s the small government payments for their land and timber ($9.70 apiece in 1896) arrived on New Year's Day and gave rise to a special holiday called Visiting Day. After collecting their payments and shooting off some celebratory rounds of gunfire, the Indian families would visit all their white neighbors—one house after the other—to sit on the floor, admire the babies, and gossip. They carried white flour sacks to bring away the cookies, cakes, pies, and fruit they were offered—for, according to Ojibway etiquette, it was rude for a guest to reject food. One early settler testified that the non-Indians "thought just as much of this occasion as the Indians did. We always dressed in our very best clothes." The Visiting Day custom was kept up as late as the 1930s, as some people still living remember.[15]

One reason the people of Grand Marais may have felt so kindly toward their Ojibway neighbors was that the Indians provided contact with the outside world. No roads, railroads, or telegraph lines reached the north shore in the nineteenth century; the mail was the main outside link. The government had established a post office at Grand Portage in 1856, but the deliveries were contracted out to local people—many of them Indians. In summer, the Superior-to-Grand Portage mail route was a two-week round trip by rowboat. One early resident wrote that "because of the possibility of bad weather, the carrier would continue his trip through much of the night. Settlements were few and far between, and should he feel the need for a rest, he would beach his boat on a convenient gravel beach and catch up on lost sleep. When the weather was rainy, he would sleep under the overturned boat, keeping a small fire alive nearby."[16]

But getting through in summer was nothing compared with the winter runs. "A dog team and sled or toboggan, traveling on the frozen lake, if the ice was safe, was the preferred transportation method. Otherwise, they mushed along the shore or through the woods, whatever was easier." The winter mail carriers became legendary. South of Grand Marais, the most famous was John Beargrease, a tall mixed-blood Ojibway from Beaver Bay. On the Grand Portage route, it was Joseph Godfrey Montferrand in the 1880s and Louis La Plante in the 1890s. Settlers along the way remembered that "in cold winter evenings the dog sled bells could be heard for miles before they arrived." In 1898, when La Plante arrived in Grand Marais just before Christmas "with his trained tandem dogs, jingling sleigh bells, U.S. mail, and toboggan, [he] resembled old Santa Claus coming to town." Starting in the 1870s the county improved the lakeshore trail so sleighs could get through, but not until 1899 was it passable for horse-drawn vehicles in summer.

Meanwhile, in the early 1880s regular summer steamer service began when the Booth company started running a fishing tug up and down the shore between Duluth and Fort William. In 1888 the *Hiram R. Dixon* was launched and soon had the summer mail contract. It made twice-weekly visits to Grand Portage till 1902, when it was replaced by the 182-foot coastal packet *America*. Such regular service made the north shore accessible not only to incoming settlers but to tourists. By 1905 the Grand Marais newspaper reported that "every passing boat has its human cargo of hay-fever fugitives, pleasure-seekers and rest-seekers."[17]

The influx of people created a demand for land. Thirty-five years after establishing the reservation, the government changed its mind and decided the best thing to do with Indian land was to sell it off. In 1887 Congress had passed the Dawes Act, designed to abolish tribally owned reservations by parceling them up into private, 160-acre tracts, or allotments. But Minnesota tribes' fates hung on an even more drastic measure, ironically titled "An act for the relief and civilization of the Chippewa Indians in the

Mail carrier on the north shore, about 1880

State of Minnesota" (usually called the Nelson Act of 1889). It decreed that all the Ojibway reservations would be wiped out and their residents resettled on the White Earth Reservation in the western part of the state. But there was a loophole. Indians who wished to take allotments in their own homeland could escape deportation. These allotments would, in theory, make their owners independent and self-supporting. Indians who chose them, though protected by government trusteeship for a time, would eventually achieve citizenship—a code word for giving up the special status of Indian identity and the rights that went with it. That year, seventy-two of the leading men of Grand Portage assembled on the bay to meet with government commissioners. With "much cheerfulness and unanimity" (or so the commissioners said), they signed a document attesting that they "do hereby grant, cede, relinquish, and convey to the United States all our right, title and interest in and to the said Grand Portage Reservation." Then they signed up for allotments that would allow them to stay precisely where they were.[18]

By 1909, some 24,191 acres of the reservation had been parceled out to 304 Indians; another 16,041 acres were slated to be opened to what was described as "public settlement." What an Ojibway was to do with 160 acres of inaccessible, rocky cutover land was a mystery. Few ever lived on their allotments; many sold them to land speculators and timber interests. The main rationale for the allotments was to give tribal members an anchor in their own land. But the system also allowed the government to sell the nonallotted land and abdicate further responsibility.[19]

Members of the Grand Portage Ojibway community with annuity goods that are stacked in front of government warehouses, 1889; Indian Agent M. A. Leahy stands at the right.

## Welcoming Visitors

In the early twentieth century, two visitors to Grand Portage left us snapshot descriptions of the community. One was an unconventional thirty-eight-year-old music teacher from southern Minnesota, Frances Densmore. Later, she would become a nationally known scholar of Indian music and culture, but her visit to Grand Portage was her first venture afield among the Indians.

Frances and her sister Margaret stepped off the Booth company steamer at Grand Marais on August 9, 1905. The first Ojibway person they met was Joe Caribou, or Iabedwaywaishkung. He was only thirty-eight, but he had been considered the leader of the Caribou clan for more than fifteen years. He may have been the grandson of Addikonse. He toured the two women around the tar-papered homes of Chippewa City and took them to meet his grandmother in her berry-picking camp. Later they met a prominent elder of the Grand Marais band, Shingibis, who was known locally as "one of the most interesting and best-liked Indian men." He gave the grave ethnologist-to-be a taste of his teasing humor. When she asked him about hunting songs, he said, "We didn't sing then. We kept *still*."[20]

Joe Caribou on the path leading to his grandmother's house, Chippewa City, 1905

It was pitch dark when the Densmores arrived at Grand Portage on a Pigeon River Lumber Company boat. The bay was too shallow for the boat to enter, so Pete Gagnon rowed out to fetch them. They stayed in Gagnon's house on the island. The village was still almost entirely Ojibway, and only the young spoke English. The Densmore sisters hired as translator Josephine Makosow, daughter of Coffee Makosow, who was one of two chiefs at the village. Frances visited the other chief, the eighty-year-old Louis Maymushkowaush, in his log home on the bay. He showed her the Franklin Pierce peace medal he had received when he signed the Treaty of 1854, as well as two British medals that had been passed down in his family.[21]

A priest from Fort William had warned Densmore that powerful non-Christian religious ceremonies were practiced at Grand Portage, so she set out to visit Menaheegonce, or Little Spruce, well known as a healer

Densmore took this photograph of Shingibis and his wife (seated at right) at Chippewa City in 1905; those standing are identified as Mrs. William Howenstine and Joe Caribou.

and member of the *Wabenowin*. Sitting in his log cabin, listening as the old man sang a song for her, Densmore observantly wrote down what she saw:

> *Hangers of twigs*
> *Herbs tied up to dry*
> *Guns on racks in two places*
> *Four clocks, all of them wrong*
> *Window held up by butcher knife*
> *Hole in floor mended with red tin*
> *Xmas* London Ill[ustrated] News
> *Deerskin folded ready to make into moccasins . . .* [22]

On August 23, members of the *Wabenowin* of Grand Portage gathered for a nighttime ceremony, feast, and vigil. They allowed Densmore to attend—although the ceremony "was not explained to me, and the Indians did not think I would attach importance to what I saw." She recorded all that she noticed—the drum with a green star on it, the drumstick in the shape of a

Menaheegonce (left) and his wife Wahzushkoonce at Grand Portage, 1905

cross, the sacred pole, the headdresses of beaver skin, the gifts and dances—but the meaning of it all was lost on her. Yet it still had an effect. "When one finds the Indian religion untouched by any shadow of doubt it cannot fail to command respect," she wrote. "This absolute fidelity to ancient traditions exists today in only a very few."

Things had changed by 1922, when another visitor arrived. Dewey Albinson was an artist from Minneapolis who traveled north in search of a wilderness to pit himself against. He was a Jack Londonesque romantic with a cynical view of human nature. He arrived at night on the steamer *America*. By now there was a dock on the island, but Pete Gagnon had moved to the mainland, leaving his buildings in the hands of one of his fishermen, a man named Rousseau. "I soon enter the house," Albinson wrote, "into a fair-sized dingy living room. A base burner is aglow. . . . The living room is as drab a setting as one can find, with the worst of mission furniture, about to give out. I settle in a battered rocker next to the stove where I can rest out the night."[23]

The next morning he had his first view of the village, "a row of white-washed log cabins near the waterfront. From each chimney rises a long, thin column of smoke against the distant dark blue mountains. I stand there entranced by the bleak beauty. I am aroused by shouts of 'Breakfast ready, breakfast ready!' I down two lard-tasting eggs, coffee, and store bread, without words."

When he crossed to the village, he found the typical dwelling to be a "French Canadian house of plain logs, with a narrow porch in front, just wide enough for a row of chairs. Here the family and visitors would line up." He stared at the older Indian women as they passed by him "in their black capes, with black handkerchiefs tied around their heads."[24]

Albinson took up lodgings with Leonard and Herman Hendrickson, Scandinavian brothers who had settled on Hat Point after the reservation was put up for sale. Leonard was "a husky blond of average build," while Herman was "a handsome rustic . . . with a vivid pink-red complexion, which makes his pale blue eyes sparkle like beads." They were fishermen. "Herman is a natural, fishing by instinct, and has an uncanny way of sensing where the fish are running. Leonard loves to read and studies the stars and other signs which he fishes by." Their Hat Point settlement consisted of "fish net reels tucked in around the sides of the cove, a log fish house with a stubby dock, a tall pole for a hoist . . . and out a little distance, a breakwater, like a protective arm." The Hendricksons both married Indian women, and today the name is a prominent one on the reservation.

Albinson had not been on the reservation long before he heard rumors of the twisted old cedar tree on Hat Point, to whose inhabiting spirit the Indians still brought gifts of tobacco. His painting of it, which he titled *The*

Dewey Albinson with
Leonard Hendrickson at
Hat Point, 1922

*Witch Tree*, was reproduced in a Minneapolis newspaper and shown in
museums around the country. Thereafter, the name of the painting was
applied to the tree itself. Many other artists later made pilgrimages to paint
the tree.[25]

There had been a generational change since Densmore's visit. The old
chief, Louis Maymushkowaush, had died and passed on the title to his
son, Joe Louis Maymushkowaush. When Joe Louis died about 1921, his
daughter's husband, Mike Flatte, claimed the hereditary chieftainship.
This succession was unorthodox, but no one challenged it. The chieftainship was largely honorary now. The real power was the U.S. Office of Indian Affairs.

The government had embarked on a crash program to eradicate the cultural boundaries that separated Indians and whites. In the first decade of
the century, it poured money and resources into an ill-conceived project to
make the Grand Portage band into farmers on their hilly, infertile allotments. At the same time it pressured the younger generation to conform
to the outside world. Many were sent away to boarding schools such as
Tomah (Wisconsin), Carlisle (Pennsylvania), Pipestone (Minnesota), Flan-
dreau (South Dakota), and the Haskell Institute (Kansas). At school they
were weaned from their native languages and cultures and instead taught
Indian history culled from sources like Longfellow's *The Song of Hiawatha*.
Even their names were taken from them. Mike Flatte told Dewey Albinson
that when he was a boy the government people came around asking everyone their names. When Flatte answered that his was Nabagadoway,
the official asked what it meant. He replied it meant "some place flat." As
Mike told it, the man said, "'O.K. . . . Call him Flat, but he gotta have another name.' Another fellow say, 'How about Mike?' 'O.K.' he say. So now

*The Cedar and the Birch* by Dewey Albinson. This representation of the "witch tree" was painted about 1940.

I be called Mike Flat." Such casual reassignments of identity were common. Many old family names were lost, and the sense of family and clan ties was weakened.[26]

Many people came to hate their Indian identity. "I no longer want to be Indian," Mike Flatte told Dewey Albinson. "I want to be white man." Others came to condemn traditional beliefs: "[Medicine] didn't help them when they were sick and needed help. Still didn't save them from their deaths." But some resisted the pressure to conform. One such couple was Alec Posey and his wife, Sangwaywaince. Posey, who had been found as an infant abandoned behind a stump, was nicknamed "Stump," signifying endurance. He was a bottomless source of tribal tradition, a member of the *Midéwiwin,* and a performer of shaking tent ceremonies. His wife, the daughter of Menaheegonce whom Densmore met, was an expert at ancient crafts such as snowshoe netting. Like many traditional doctors, Posey was a counselor as well as a curer, a source of community morale. "He was such a nice man," one Grand Portage resident recalled in 1962. "I still think he helped me in a lot of ways with his medicine. I just loved that man to pieces. We all felt that way."[27]

By the mid-1920s an all-weather road, Minnesota Trunk Highway 1, was open between Duluth and Fort William. It ran four miles inland from the village, but it still brought a new resource to replace the timber: tourists. Soon the highway was dotted with "Indian curio" shops that sold souvenirs to passing motorists and provided income to craft workers. At the border crossing, Sextus Lindahl opened a beer tavern, restaurant, and cabins. A settlement grew up around a general store at Mineral Center, where the dirt road to Grand Portage took off from the highway. Soon visitors were finding their way to the village on the bay.[28]

The former Grand Portage schoolteacher, Effie Falconer McLean, who had been born on Susie Island, now became the village entrepreneur. After Pete Gagnon's death in 1935, she bought his trading post—"for a few hundred dollars and an old car," said Dewey Albinson. Near the store she built some tourist cabins equipped with wood stoves, outdoor toilets, and an electric generator for lights. A former lumber-camp cook provided "heavy-duty" meals in a nearby dining room. Soon the McLean Resort was full of city people come to fish, hunt, and enjoy the rustic life for two dollars a day. Even more traffic was generated when some Duluthians organized Lucky Star Landing to run motor boats over to Isle Royale from Grand Portage.

The Grand Portage band's relationship with the government changed yet again in the 1930s. The administration of Franklin D. Roosevelt decided to reverse the old policy of forced assimilation in favor of self-determination. But it was not a return to the old days. The Indian Reorganization Act of 1934 gave tribes the option of organizing themselves into self-governing bodies based on the Euro-American model of representative democracy. In Minnesota this led to a proposal for forming an entity called the Minnesota Chippewa Tribe to represent the Ojibway with outside organizations like the state and federal governments. It would include elected representatives from all the state's reservations. In 1937 the Grand Portage band joined the new Minnesota Chippewa Tribe. Only the Red Lake band declined. Thereafter, the people of Grand Portage belonged to two entities called the Chippewa tribe—a legal and governmental body that included neither all Ojibway nor all in Minnesota, and an older tribe with bonds of language, culture, and kinship that spanned state and national boundaries but had no legal existence.[29]

Locally, the band also formed a new governing body—the Grand Portage Reservation Council, later called the Reservation Business Committee. It functioned much like a county government, handling all matters not concerning other reservations. One of its first acts was to establish a co-op store for residents.

Because it had reversed its policy on abolishing reservations, the government returned the unsold portions of land around Grand Portage to the Indians. Part went to the local band and part to the Minnesota Chippewa Tribe, creating a land-ownership patchwork of Byzantine complexity. Soon the band, with government assistance, began buying back privately owned tracts lost during allotment. By 1990, 79 percent of the reservation was tribally owned—a high percentage in Minnesota.[30]

The 1930s brought an influx of government money unheard of since the 1870s. The Civilian Conservation Corps, Works Progress Administration, and Civil Works Administration all provided employment: forestry projects, road building, community improvement, even crafts projects. All this activity had a major impact on the geography of the village, which had always been oriented toward the water. Now, the government set to work "clearing out the worst of the old buildings which cluttered up the main village area adjacent to the water front" in order to restore its "primitive setting." The new frame homes built inland were oriented toward the roads. A new school and a community hall were erected on the ridge behind the old village site. To fit the rustic theme, they were built of logs—but the logs, imported from Oregon, were square-cut and had to be rounded again by hand in order to look like logs![31]

The changes were not to everyone's liking. Dewey Albinson remembered meeting an old Indian woman on Mount Rose, looking out over the valley. "She is crying. She had returned to her place of birth to visit her friends, only to find the places dear to her memory gone, gone, never to be recovered." But others didn't think the development had gone nearly far enough. In the 1930s a new controversy arose. The immediate issue was a new road, but the divisive question really was economic development versus preservation of old lifeways.[32]

The state of Minnesota wanted to build a new road up the north shore, U.S. Highway 61. The first route proposed would have been disastrous—through the center of the village, then across the Pigeon at the spectacular High Falls. A coalition set out to block it: conservation groups like the Izaak Walton League of America and the Quetico-Superior Council teamed up with the secretary of the interior, whose main objective was preservation of the Indian community.[33]

The charge made at the time was that the main backers of the road were investors in Duluth and Grand Marais who had bought up lakeshore property on the reservation, anticipating that the value would soar if the road went through. Whatever the truth of the allegation, it was Duluth businessmen who lobbied hardest for the road. The reservation council, dominated by prodevelopment forces, came out in favor of the proposal. "The Indians feel that they do not want to be isolated," testified the attorney for the Minnesota Chippewa Tribe. "They want the whites to come to them. They do not want to be located at any dead-end street."

In the end it was not the conservationists that killed the road, but World War II. After the war the idea was revived, with changes: the highway would skirt the village on the north and leave the High Falls alone. The road was finally finished in 1966.[34]

A government commission that visited Grand Portage at the height of the road controversy left a view of life there in 1941. About 199 Ojibway people lived on the reservation, 100 more at Grand Marais. They supported themselves mainly by commercial fishing but also by hunting, trapping, guiding, handicrafts, and government work. A quarter of their food came from gardens and hunting. Despite the new frame cottages with shingled sides and roofs built during the Great Depression, a typical home was still "a pole frame dwelling covered with tar paper, one or two rooms, four windows, single floor, no storm doors or windows." Between 75 and 90 percent of the people were Catholic, but most still used traditional medicines. Euro-American medicine was available only once a week when a doctor and a nurse visited from Grand Marais. The government noted that "practically all of the middle-aged and the younger Indians endeavor to dress, talk, and act like white people."

## Uncovering the Past

In 1922 Solon J. Buck, director of the Minnesota Historical Society in St. Paul, received an alarming letter from a resident of Grand Portage. Many age-old rights of way on the reservation were being bought up, fenced, and posted. The old Grand Portage trail itself had been marked "closed."[35]

Concerned for the preservation of the historic sites at Grand Portage, Buck sent the society's field representative and a newspaper reporter to retrace the old trail. The resulting publicity roused public interest, and so Buck hired Dewey Albinson to make a systematic survey of the sites. Albinson, with a local crew, set off up the trail.

The portage was obstructed by fallen trees, but its route was still plain. In some places wagon ruts were visible. In others, Albinson said, "the old heavily trodden earth was so like a cushion that a blind man could follow it." When the crew reached Fort Charlotte, it found an old cellar hole and the remains of the dock along the riverbank. "Running back alongside a creek bed was a straight ridge, like one made by a plow, obviously the line of the former stockade," Albinson reported. He and his helpers cleared the dense underbrush, revealing more building outlines and cellar holes, which they mapped.[36]

The time was right to save Grand Portage's fur trade history. Public interest in the subject was high as a result of popularizations like *The Voyageur* by historian Grace Lee Nute. Moreover, conservationists were lobbying to preserve the boundary lakes as a wilderness canoe area. Buck's first idea was to promote a Fort Charlotte State Park, but the crazy quilt of federal and Indian land ownership in the area soon scotched the idea.[37]

Depression-era relief agencies finally got the ball rolling—a little too fast, in fact. In February 1936, to everyone's surprise, the Civilian Conservation Corps allocated $6,200 for reconstructing a portion of the North West Company depot at Grand Portage. The money had to be spent by June, the end of the fiscal year. The Office of Indian Affairs appealed to the Minnesota Historical Society, which insisted on an archaeological investigation before the site was touched. A funding extension was worked out, and archaeologist Ralph D. Brown arrived later that year to start excavations with a crew of local Ojibway men.[38]

On the depot site was a log cabin, two fish houses, and two barns, and the main road ran across the southern part of it. On the surface, little of the original post was visible: two furrows marking stretches of the north and west stockades and some scattered piles of boulders where chimneys had collapsed. The archaeologists laid out a checkerboard of exploratory trenches and soon ran into stockade lines. To their joy, they found the bases of more than a dozen pickets standing in position, sandwiched between horizontal support beams. The wood was later identified as white cedar. They also uncovered one spike-topped picket more than eleven feet long, plus a horizontal crossbar and pegs that had fastened the pickets together near the top. The main gate, which they had expected to face the lakeshore, turned up on the northeast side, next to the creek.[39]

The next year's investigations proved even more interesting. On a low ridge running across the center of the depot was the stone foundation of the Great Hall. West of it lay the remains of a typical trader's lodging with two fireplaces. East of it they found a cellar containing a complete plank door and fragments of walls constructed in French fashion with hand-hewn boards fitted into grooved upright posts. North of the Great Hall, the well, lined with eighteenth-century barrels, yielded a cedar shingle, a wooden bucket, and samples of the "Spanish brown" paint used on buildings. By the end of two seasons, the archaeologists had located all the stockade lines, including two that unexpectedly partitioned off the depot interior; the potential remains of thirteen structures; and hundreds of artifacts revealing the world of cheap, ready-made goods the traders inhabited: clay pipe fragments, bottle glass, earthenware, pewter, spigots, buttons, knives, lead balls, gun pieces, trade rings, files, chisels, hinges, and nails.

The reconstruction started in 1938. The palisades were erected again in the original trenches, and a rustic pioneer-style building rose on the Great Hall foundations. One end was devoted to a coffee and souvenir shop run by the Grand Portage band, while the other held museum cases full of historic artifacts and contemporary crafts donated by band members. This was the only building completed when World War II broke out, federal funds dried up, and Grand Portage was "literally abandoned" by all but the Ojibway.[40]

By the 1950s the depot was a pitiful sight: the palisade was rotted and falling, the Great Hall was leaking, weatherbeaten, and neglected. The Grand Portage band, lacking funds and fed up with seeing the tourism potential of the site wasted, turned to the National Park Service for help. It was a logical choice. Nearby Isle Royale was administered by the park service, and advocates of a major national park along the boundary saw Grand Portage as a springboard for their scheme. The first step was tentative: in 1951 the U.S. Department of the Interior designated Grand Portage a National Historic Site—a status sometimes given to sites before making

The first reconstruction of the North West Company depot at Grand Portage, shown here in 1951

them national parks—and agreed to provide the band with "technical assistance limited by available funding" to operate it.

The arrangement did not turn on the federal money spigot. Reluctantly, the reservation council came to a hard decision: the band would have to cede the land to the federal government in order to get the site developed. In 1958 Congress approved the unusual transfer, and in 1960 Grand Portage National Monument was formally established. The first park superintendent arrived that year, charged with "major restoration projects to transform the monument to its appearance 200 years ago."[41]

The lack of written sources on Grand Portage soon became apparent, making more archaeology critical. In 1961, in a cooperative agreement with the Minnesota Historical Society, archaeologist Alan R. Woolworth arrived to start what would become a fifteen-year project of excavations. Together with his historian wife, Nancy, and two young daughters, Woolworth soon came up against the cultural politics of living and working in an Indian community. Employing almost exclusively local band members, he had to make adjustments not unlike those of fur traders two hundred years before.[42]

Many of the excavations funded in the 1960s and 1970s were salvage projects made necessary by planned construction. Thus, to the archaeologists' frustration, the dig sites were often chosen not for their likelihood of yielding information, but for their suitability for sewers, buildings, and utility lines. At first, attention was directed across the creek from the depot. In 1961 three teams of archaeologists dug test pits north and east of Grand Portage Creek, finding the sites of several Office of Indian Affairs buildings from the late nineteenth and early twentieth centuries and what was probably a historic Ojibway dwelling. The next year the focus shifted closer to Lake Superior, where the National Park Service wanted to build an interpretive center—an idea that was quickly abandoned when four nineteenth-century Ojibway burials were found on the site. Digging three thousand feet of trenches, the archaeologists also uncovered several more Indian Affairs buildings, a turn-of-the-century log cabin, and a prehistoric projectile point. In 1975 they returned to the area and found traces of a fenced enclosure, a possible stone and clay fireplace, and some enigmatic structure sites near the road.

In 1963–64 and 1969 the projects that drove the archaeology were the replacement of the palisades and installation of the modern sewer and water lines for public facilities. The entire palisade line was excavated and a more accurate interpretation of the main gate worked out. A warehouse building was found outside the palisades (the present canoe warehouse). In 1970–71 the Great Hall was excavated again, this time turning up evidence of its porch. Historians had postulated a kitchen behind it, based

Excavating the Great Hall, 1970. Ruins of fireplaces lie at each end of the structure.

on the layout of Fort William, and, sure enough, the outline of a square building surrounded by porches was found. The kitchen yielded almost 14,500 artifacts, including food remains that showed an unexpected dependence on domestic animals and eating utensils that reflected the formal manners, class structure, and international tone of fur trade society. Also found were the remains of a fireplace, apparently last used to burn a pile of furniture, and a small stone-lined dry well or cooler with its wooden floor still in place. A dozen or more building sites still await systematic excavation. Such archaeological treasure troves as trash pits and latrines have yet to be found.

Meanwhile, more research was going on at Fort Charlotte. The Minnesota Historical Society, which was sponsoring an underwater archaeology project along the border lakes, decided in 1972 to investigate the bottom of the Pigeon River. Archaeologist Douglas A. Birk was told to organize an expedition, and hardy crew members backpacked heavy equipment to the site along the rain-slick portage through clouds of mosquitoes. They proceeded to map, then literally vacuum, the mucky river bottom. A land team strained the mud for artifacts while a river team fought aggressive leeches that slithered inside wet suits and even divers' mouths. Unlike the depot on the bay, which was mainly yielding artifacts of the 1770s to 1790s, the river held everything from early French ceramics to modern camping debris. Wooden canoe parts, keg lids, and leather shoes had been preserved in the anaerobic sludge. By mapping the distribution of datable artifacts, Birk was able to show that the landing area had shifted upriver over its years of use, ending at the still-preserved remains of the North West Company dock.[43]

On the rainy dawn of July 15, 1969, a tremendous clap of thunder shook Grand Portage village. Two campers who had taken shelter in the depot's gatehouse saw fire where lightning had struck the roof of the Great Hall, and they spread the alarm. As a local resident told it, "A sleepy throng gathers. Frantic efforts are made to bring pumps and hose into position. The fire spreads. Clouds of dirty black smoke begin to pour from the great stone chimneys. It is too late. . . . People stand in little groups watching quietly as the flames reach ever higher toward the gray morning skies. There is the feeling of a funeral and a sad farewell to a grand old building."[44]

The 1938–40 reconstruction of the Great Hall was a total loss. Dewey Albinson's original *Witch Tree* painting and many early Ojibway artifacts were destroyed. But the fire did give the National Park Service the opportunity to rebuild, this time basing the design on historical research. The work, much of it laborious hand hewing, was done by local residents. The new building opened in 1974, and four years later a reconstructed kitchen was added, bringing the site to a new level of authenticity.[45]

A diver conducting underwater archaeology at the site of Fort Charlotte in 1972 finds a brass teakettle.

Today, Grand Portage is a place where everyone carries around a few internal boundaries—boundaries between past and present, between cultures, between world views. Conflicting goals pull and tug at each other across the borders: the desire to attract tourists but preserve the seclusion, to use resources but protect the environment, to have jobs and well-being but keep old values strong. Living in Grand Portage is a balancing act, a precarious walk through a maze of boundaries.

The business savvy that the band has shown since the 1730s began to pay off in the 1970s. The Reservation Business Committee became the sparkplug for development of tribal ventures. The first experiment, a maple sugar processing plant, failed after two years due to problems with transportation, seasonality, and cost. But plans based on the ancient Ojibway custom of hospitality succeeded. A multimillion-dollar tourist facility was planned, its keystone the Grand Portage Lodge and Conference Center. This hotel complex, built with federal grants and band dollars, opened in 1975. It was at first run in cooperation with the Radisson hotel chain, but the band took over its operation in 1980 and added a marina, campgrounds, and ski trails. After gaming was introduced in 1990, it was renamed the Grand Portage Lodge and Casino. Each summer Grand Portage plays host

Site interpreters Karen Evens and Don Carney inside the Great Hall, 1985

to a rush of passing travelers, as it has done for more than two hundred years.[46]

Logging was resumed in the late 1970s, this time under Indian control. The Reservation Business Committee developed a comprehensive forest management plan that balances the needs of wildlife, recreation, maple sugaring, and timber harvesting. The local store, called the Trading Post, is run as a co-op by the band. Acting in its role as a local government, the business committee has also sought out money for home improvements (central heating was almost unknown on the reservation before the 1960s), roads, sewers, water lines, an ambulance, and fire protection. In many ways, Grand Portage is becoming a successful, self-reliant reservation.

Which is not to say there are not problems. It is particularly hard to balance economic progress against preservation of Ojibway language and culture. The younger generation sometimes feels alienated from the past. One teenager said, "My father says he thinks there are people in Grand Portage today who would be real ashamed to speak out and do the old ways. . . . Maybe they think it's going out of style. Like the clothes. Everyone wants to keep up with the new style, and they're ashamed of the old

The Grand Portage Lodge and Casino, about 1990

The promise of the future radiates from the faces of Ojibway children like David Novitsky of Grand Portage, shown gathering blueberries in 1987.

stuff." "It's just gone away," another teenager said. "All the people that did it are real old. . . . That was all long ago."[47]

James Hull, a longtime Grand Portage resident, expressed the conflict best: "To the older Indians of the Grand Portage Reservation, it is a tranquil, protected island of refuge surrounded by a turbulent sea of modern progress and feverish quest. It is a peaceful place where life is simple and unhurried, where wood smoke still perfumes the night air, and where an Indian can still be an Indian if he chooses. . . . To the younger Indian . . . Grand Portage is a hope for compromise wherein progress and opportunity might be brought to the Reservation to provide the kind of life which he, as an American, has a right to earn and enjoy. . . .

"In its essence then, Grand Portage is a puzzle and a challenge."[48]

As it always has been.

# Notes

The following abbreviations have been used in the notes:

| | |
|---|---|
| AETS | American Exploration and Travel Series |
| *CHR* | *Canadian Historical Review* |
| CPA | Canada, Public Archives (renamed the National Archives of Canada) |
| *DCB* | *Dictionary of Canadian Biography* |
| FWJ | Fort William Journals |
| GPLCC | Grand Portage Local Curriculum Committee |
| GPNM | Grand Portage National Monument, Grand Portage, Minn. |
| GPO | U.S. Government Printing Office |
| *MH* | *Minnesota History* |
| MHS | Minnesota Historical Society, St. Paul |
| *MPHC* | *Michigan Pioneer and Historical Collections* |
| NPS | U.S. Dept. of the Interior, National Park Service |
| OIA | U.S. Office of Indian Affairs |
| PCS | Publications of the Champlain Society |
| *WHC* | *Wisconsin Historical Collections* |

## Chapter 1. The Boundary of East and West

1. Richard W. Ojakangas and Charles L. Matsch, *Minnesota's Geology* (Minneapolis: University of Minnesota Press, 1982), 50–51, 176.

2. Norval Morriseau, *Legends of My People, the Great Ojibway*, ed. Selwyn Dewdney (Toronto: Ryerson Press, 1965), 4–6, 22–32; Daniel Williams Harmon, *Sixteen Years in the Indian Country: The Journal of Daniel Williams Harmon, 1800–1816*, ed. W. Kaye Lamb (Toronto: Macmillan Co. of Canada, 1957), 230; John Johnston, "An Account of Lake Superior, 1792–1807," in *Les Bourgeois de la Compagnie du Nord-Ouest*, ed. Louis R. Masson (1889–90; reprint, New York: Antiquarian Press, 1960), 2:153; GPLCC, *A History of*

*Kitchi Onigaming: Grand Portage and Its People* (Cass Lake, Minn.: Minnesota Chippewa Tribe, 1983), 75. A good example of a prayer said by Ojibway travelers on Lake Superior is in John Tanner, *A Narrative of the Captivity and Adventures of John Tanner* (1830; reprint, Minneapolis: Ross & Haines, 1956), 25.

3. OIA, *Report of the Commissioner* (Washington, D.C.), 1878, p. 147, 1880, p. 173, 1882, p. 176.

4. On the layout of the campsites, see Alan R. and Nancy L. Woolworth, "Grand Portage National Monument: An Historical Overview and an Inventory of Its Cultural Resources," 1982, vol. 1:164–69, typescript in MHS. The cemetery site is inferred from the discovery of some fur-trade-era human remains when the foundations of the present school were being dug; see "Grand Portage National Monument" 2: structure/feature no. 91. Tanner, *Narrative,* 22, indicates that both Indians and whites used it. For the numbers present in summer, see Grace Lee Nute, ed., "A British Legal Case and Old Grand Portage," *MH* 21 (June 1940): 140.

5. Harmon, *Sixteen Years,* 47; Alexander Henry (the Younger), *The Journal of Alexander Henry the Younger, 1799–1814,* ed. Barry M. Gough, PCS, 56 (Toronto: Champlain Society, 1988), 1:1; John Macdonell, "The Diary of John Macdonell," in *Five Fur Traders of the Northwest,* ed. Charles M. Gates (St. Paul: MHS, 1965), 93.

6. George Nelson, "A Winter in the St. Croix Valley, 1802–03," ed. Richard Bardon and Grace Lee Nute, *MH* 28 (Mar., June, Sept. 1947): 7.

7. Alexander Mackenzie, *The Journals and Letters of Sir Alexander Mackenzie,* ed. W. Kaye Lamb (Cambridge: Cambridge University Press, 1970), 98–99; Macdonell, "Diary," 95; Nelson, "Winter," 12; Alexander Henry, *Travels and Adventures in Canada and the Indian Territories between the Years 1760 and 1776,* ed. James Bain (Boston: Little, Brown, 1901), 55. There were two traders named Alexander Henry. This one was later dubbed "the Elder" to distinguish him from his nephew, called "the Younger." Unless otherwise specified, all citations here are to Henry the Elder.

8. Harold A. Innis, *The Fur Trade in Canada: An Introduction to Canadian Economic History,* rev. ed. (Toronto: University of Toronto Press, 1956), 240.

9. The contrast between the camps is extrapolated from later descriptions of Fort William; see Gabriel Franchère, *Journal of a Voyage on the North West Coast of North America during the Years 1811, 1812, 1813 and 1814,* trans. Wessie Tipping Lamb, ed. W. Kaye Lamb, PCS, 45 (Toronto: Champlain Society, 1969), 181; Joseph Delafield, *The Unfortified Boundary,* ed. Robert McElroy and Thomas Riggs (New York: Privately published, 1943), 401. The quotations refer to Grand Portage; see A. Mackenzie, *Journals and Letters,* 98, and Nute, ed., "Legal Case," 140.

10. A. Mackenzie, *Journals and Letters,* 97; Willard Ferdinand Wentzel, "Letters to the Hon. Roderic [*sic*] McKenzie, 1807–1824," in *Les Bourgeois,* ed. Masson, 1:71; John J. Bigsby, *The Shoe and Canoe; or, Pictures of Travel in the Canadas* (London: Chapman & Hall, 1850), 1:147; Henry, *Travels and Adventures,* 34–35, 154.

11. A. Mackenzie, *Journal and Letters,* 97–98; Innis, *Fur Trade,* 227.

12. Nute, ed., "Legal Case," 131, 146–48. For a discussion of where Lecuyer's (later Boucher's) fort stood, see A. and N. Woolworth, "Grand Portage National Monument" 1:160–63.

13. Nute, ed., "Legal Case," 147.

14. A. Mackenzie, *Journals and Letters,* 94, 484, 497; Harmon, *Sixteen Years,* 19, 20; Macdonell, "Diary," 94, 96; Erwin N. Thompson, *Grand Portage: A History of the Sites, People, and Fur Trade* (Washington, D.C.: NPS, Office of Archeology and Historic Preservation, Division of History, 1969), 93–94, 100. The second wharf was built between 1793, when Macdonell didn't mention it, and 1799, when William McGillivray did. A. and N. Woolworth proposed that it may have been on the island, where a pier was located in the twentieth century; see "Grand Portage National Monument" 1:92–93. At least one of the rowboats was big enough to tow the *Otter,* as Macdonell mentioned.

15. Macdonell, "Diary," 92.

16. Bigsby, *Shoe and Canoe* 2:218–19; George Thomas Landmann, *Adventures and Recollections of Colonel Landmann* (London: Colburn & Co., 1852), 1:305–6.

17. Landmann, *Adventures and Recollections* 1:303–4; Innis, *Fur Trade*, 214, 216; A. Mackenzie, *Journals and Letters*, 84–85.

18. Harmon, *Sixteen Years*, 21; Nelson, "Winter," 142.

19. Daniel Williams Harmon, *A Journal of Voyages and Travels in the Interior of North America* (1820; reprint, Toronto: Courier Press, 1911), 15; Macdonell, "Diary," 93; George Heriot, *Travels through the Canadas* (London: Richard Phillips, 1807), 204.

20. Macdonell, "Diary," 94; Harmon, *Sixteen Years*, 20.

21. For the cooper, see E. Thompson, *Grand Portage*, 93. The blacksmith was mentioned by A. Mackenzie, *Journals and Letters*, 487.

22. Innis, *Fur Trade*, 210, 227; E. Thompson, *Grand Portage*, 90; Harmon, *Sixteen Years*, 21–22.

23. A. Mackenzie, *Journals and Letters*, 82.

24. Henry, *Travels and Adventures*, 320.

25. A. and N. Woolworth, "Grand Portage National Monument" 1:115–18. William McGillivray mentioned the powder house in 1800; see E. Thompson, *Grand Portage*, 100–101. Its location is not known.

26. Harmon, *Sixteen Years*, 22–23; Nelson, "Winter," 8; René Thomas Verchères de Boucherville, "Journal of Thomas Verchères de Boucherville," in *War on the Detroit*, ed. Milo Milton Quaife, Lakeside Classics, no. 38 (Chicago: Lakeside Press, 1940), 5.

27. Innis, *Fur Trade*, 243; A. Mackenzie, *Journals and Letters*, 458. For currencies in use at Grand Portage, see Nute, ed., "Legal Case," 125, 131, 146. Traders were inconsistent as to whether the units of Grand Portage currency were called pounds or livres, but their value is consistently given as twelve GPC to one pound Halifax. See Henry (the Younger), *Journal*, 129n121; Macdonell, "Diary," 93–94; Archibald N. McLeod, "The Diary of Archibald N. McLeod," and Hugh Faries, "The Diary of Hugh Faries"—both in *Five Fur Traders*, ed. Gates, 132, 240; Roderick McKenzie, "Reminiscences," in *Les Bourgeois*, ed. Masson, 1:61–66.

28. A. Mackenzie, *Journals and Letters*, 98, 492.

29. Where they met is pure speculation; at Fort William there was a special council house. See Old Fort William, Thunder Bay, Ontario, "Old Fort William at a Glance: A Thematic Guide to Old Fort William Structures and Their Functions" (n.d., training manual), 28.

30. A good example of the kinds of information exchanged is Alexander Mackenzie's letter of June 4, 1799, in *Journals and Letters*, 474–83.

31. For examples of lobbying, see A. Mackenzie, *Journals and Letters*, 452, 454–55.

32. Innis, *Fur Trade*, 210, 244. This paragraph is based on 1799, when William McGillivray and Alexander Mackenzie were at Grand Portage during the months cited.

33. Harmon, *Sixteen Years*, 22; A. and N. Woolworth, "Grand Portage National Monument" 1:181–82.

34. A. Mackenzie, *Journals and Letters*, 97. The evidence for pigs is archaeological; see Alan R. Woolworth, "Archaeological Excavations at the North West Company's Depot, Grand Portage, Minnesota, in 1970–1971 by the Minnesota Historical Society," 1975, p. 276, typescript in MHS. Despite Alexander Mackenzie's pessimistic views on agriculture at Grand Portage, William McGillivray in 1800 instructed the post manager to plow ground and plant crops east of the creek; E. Thompson, *Grand Portage*, 92. It is not known where the barn was located; it may have been outside the depot.

35. Bigsby, *Shoe and Canoe* 1:145; Delafield, *Unfortified Boundary*, 405. The quotations are from J. Johnston, "Account of Lake Superior," 165, and A. Mackenzie, *Journals and Letters*, 97.

36. Macdonell, "Diary," 97; Harmon, *Sixteen Years*, 12. The Harmon quotation does not refer specifically to the Grand Portage.

37. A. Mackenzie, *Journals and Letters*, 97. Nute, ed., "Legal Case," 139, said that in 1803 the public road ran "from the Beach to the little River" (presumably Pigeon River), or from the forts on the bay "to the North side of the Portage." The witness assumed it was built by the North West Company. When John Tanner crossed the portage about 1795,

wagons seem to have been the preferred mode of transportation on "the trader's road"; see his *Narrative*, 51.

38. Henry, *Travels and Adventures*, 236; Henry (the Younger), *Journal* 1:5; Delafield, *Unfortified Boundary*, 404; Bigsby, *Shoe and Canoe* 2:241–42. For a detailed survey of the sources on the trail, see A. and N. Woolworth, "Grand Portage National Monument" 1:47–68. None of the poses or landmarks has yet been identified.

39. Henry, *Travels and Adventures*, 230, 236; David Thompson, *David Thompson's Narrative, 1784–1812*, ed. Richard Glover, PCS, no. 40 (Toronto: Champlain Society, 1962), 137; "Letter of Benjamin and Joseph Frobisher to General Haldimand, Dated October 4, 1784," in *Documents Relating to the North West Company*, ed. W. Stewart Wallace, PCS, no. 22 (Toronto: Champlain Society, 1934), 73.

40. Heriot, *Travels*, 205; John McDonald (sometimes spelled MacDonald) of Garth, quoted in Duncan McGillivray, *The Journal of Duncan M'Gillivray of the North West Company at Fort George on the Saskatchewan, 1794–5*, ed. Arthur S. Morton (Toronto: Macmillan Co. of Canada, 1929), lii. For a detailed summary of sources on Fort Charlotte, see A. and N. Woolworth, "Grand Portage National Monument" 1:69–78. Underwater archaeology was done in the Pigeon River opposite Fort Charlotte, but neither of the two fort sites has been excavated; see Robert C. Wheeler et al., *Voices from the Rapids: An Underwater Search for Fur Trade Artifacts, 1960–73*, Minnesota Historical Archaeology Series, no. 3 (St. Paul: MHS, 1975), 85–93.

41. Innis, *Fur Trade*, 227–28; A. Mackenzie, *Journals and Letters*, 99; Macdonell, "Diary," 97.

42. D. Thompson, *Narrative*, 137; Innis, *Fur Trade*, 228; Henry (the Younger), *Journal* 1:6–7. For an example of mix-ups on the portages, see Macdonell, "Diary," 98.

43. A. Mackenzie, *Journals and Letters*, 98.

44. John McDonald of Garth, "Autobiographical Notes, 1791–1816," in *Les Bourgeois*, ed. Masson, 2:18. Use of a dinner bell is inferred from Alexander Ross, *The Fur Hunters of the Far West*, ed. Kenneth A. Spaulding, AETS, no. 20 (Norman: University of Oklahoma Press, 1956), 19.

45. A. Mackenzie, *Journals and Letters*, 98; Bigsby, *Shoe and Canoe* 2:231; Ross, *Fur Hunters*, 18–20. There are no surviving descriptions of a meal at Grand Portage. Bigsby described one at Fort William and Ross one at Fort George on the Columbia River, but the system at Grand Portage was probably similar. The phrase on the *bourgeois'* dress describes Duncan Cameron at his inland post; again, it is reasonable to suppose that dress codes at Grand Portage were similarly formal. See Shirlee A. Smith, "James Sutherland: Inland Trader, 1751–1797," *The Beaver*, Winter 1975, p. 21.

46. A. Woolworth, "Archaeological Excavations . . . 1970–1971," p. 158–66, 220–25, 247–48; A. Mackenzie, *Journals and Letters*, 98, 487; McDonald of Garth, "Autobiographical Notes," 15.

47. Ross, *Fur Hunters*, 20; Harmon, *Sixteen Years*, 25–26, 119.

48. Harmon, *Sixteen Years*, 22.

49. R. McKenzie, "Reminiscences," 12, refers to the grand lodge. He was the only fur trader who mentioned the Indian village, much less described it. We do not know where it was located. This description is based on Frances Densmore's *Chippewa Customs* (1929; reprint, St. Paul: MHS Press, Borealis Books, 1979), and on Eastman Johnson's paintings of the village in 1857; see Patricia Condon Johnston, *Eastman Johnson's Lake Superior Indians* (Afton, Minn.: Johnston Publishing, 1983).

50. On fur traders collecting souvenirs, see R. McKenzie, "Reminiscences," 36; on topics of conversation, see Henry, *Travels and Adventures*, 148.

## Chapter 2. First Contact

1. William W. Warren, *History of the Ojibway People* (1885; reprint, St. Paul: MHS Press, Borealis Books, 1984), 83. Warren spelled the latter word, more correctly, as *Naudowasewug*; given here is the French spelling, which evolved into the name Sioux.

2. Louise Phelps Kellogg, "The French Regime in the Great Lakes Country," *MH* 12 (Dec. 1931): 349; Pierre Gaultier de Varennes, sieur de La Vérendrye, *Journals and Letters of Pierre Gaultier de Varennes de la Vérendrye and His Sons,* ed. Lawrence J. Burpee, PCS, no. 16 (Toronto: Champlain Society, 1927), 34.

3. Nicolas Perrot, "Memoir on the Manners, Customs, and Religion of the Savages of North America," in *The Indian Tribes of the Upper Mississippi Valley and Region of the Great Lakes,* trans. and ed. Emma Helen Blair (Cleveland: Arthur H. Clark Co., 1911), 1:43; Pierre Esprit, sieur de Radisson, "Radisson's Account of His Third Journey, 1658–1660 [1654–1656?]," in *Early Narratives of the Northwest, 1634–1699,* ed. Louise Phelps Kellogg, Original Narratives of Early American History (New York: Charles Scribner's Sons, 1917), 46–47; Harmon, *Sixteen Years,* 199; Conrad E. Heidenreich and Arthur J. Ray, *The Early Fur Trades: A Study in Cultural Interaction,* New Canadian Geography Project, Historical Patterns Series (Toronto: McClelland & Stewart, 1976), 13.

4. Innis, *Fur Trade,* 33.

5. Heidenreich and Ray, *Early Fur Trades,* 16–17.

6. Paul C. Thistle, *Indian-European Trade Relations in the Lower Saskatchewan River Region to 1840,* Manitoba Studies in Native History, no. 2 (Winnipeg: University of Manitoba Press, 1986), passim; Innis, *Fur Trade,* 80, 117; Wentzel, "Letters," 96. For more on the loaded semantics of "laziness," see Mary Black-Rogers, "'Starving' and Survival in the Subarctic Fur Trade: A Case for Contextual Semantics," in *"Le Castor Fait Tout": Selected Papers of the Fifth North American Fur Trade Conference, 1985,* ed. Bruce G. Trigger et al. (Montreal: Lake St. Louis Historical Society, 1987), 633–35.

7. Thistle, *Trade Relations,* 18–19; Harold Hickerson, *The Chippewa and Their Neighbors: A Study in Ethnohistory,* rev. and expanded ed. (Prospect Heights, Ill.: Waveland Press, 1988), 122; Harmon, *Sixteen Years,* 79, 87.

8. Warren, *History of the Ojibway People,* 269; Bruce M. White, "'Give Us a Little Milk': The Social and Cultural Meanings of Gift Giving in the Lake Superior Fur Trade," *MH* 48 (Summer 1982): 60–71. *Canada* is used throughout this volume for the sake of continuity. While under French rule, the territory was known as New France.

9. Innis, *Fur Trade,* 21; La Vérendrye, *Journals and Letters,* 149; White, "'Give Us a Little Milk,'" 60–71, and "A Skilled Game of Exchange: Ojibway Fur Trade Protocol," *MH* 50 (Summer 1987): 229–40.

10. Perrot, "Memoir," 160–63. *Jawendjige* was Father Frederic Baraga's spelling in his *A Dictionary of the Otchipwe Language, Explained in English* (1878; reprint, Minneapolis: Ross & Haines, 1966), part 2, p. 167. Warren, *History of the Ojibway People,* 64, used *shah-wau-je-gay.* For more on this concept, see Black-Rogers, "'Starving' and Survival," 638–42.

11. Charles Claude le Roy, sieur Bacqueville de La Potherie, "Adventures of Nicolas Perrot, by La Potherie, 1665–1670," in *Early Narratives,* ed. Kellogg, 82; Thistle, *Trade Relations,* 47; Innis, *Fur Trade,* 32.

12. La Potherie, "Adventures of Nicolas Perrot," 77, 86–87.

13. La Potherie, "Adventures of Nicolas Perrot," 81; Innis, *Fur Trade,* 18, 172. For an extended discussion of the issue of dependence, see Thistle, *Trade Relations.* Traders made many of the claims of dependence when reporting on trade rhetoric, where the Indians were attempting to arouse "pity," and in polemical documents, where traders were trying to convince government officials they were performing a public service.

14. Warren, *History of the Ojibway People,* 131–32; "The Pageant of 1671," in *Early Narratives,* ed. Kellogg, 211–20.

15. Hickerson, *Chippewa and Their Neighbors,* 37.

16. Innis, *Fur Trade,* 29, 55.

17. Innis, *Fur Trade,* 45, 52.

18. Here and below, see Perrot, "Memoir," 173–74; Louise Phelps Kellogg, *The French Régime in Wisconsin and the Northwest* (Madison: State Historical Society of Wisconsin, 1925), 163; Johanna E. Feest and Christian F. Feest, "Ottawa," in *Northeast,* ed. Bruce G. Trigger, vol. 15 in *Handbook of North American Indians,* ed. William C. Sturtevant (Washington, D.C.: Smithsonian Institution, 1978), 773.

19. This, at least, is the interpretation of ethnohistorian Harold Hickerson, in *The*

*Southwestern Chippewa: An Ethnohistorical Study,* American Anthropological Association, Memoir 92 (Menasha, Wis., 1962), 72–80, and *Chippewa and Their Neighbors,* 42–45. See also Warren, *History of the Ojibway People,* 44, 45, 164; E. S. Rogers, "Southeastern Ojibwa," in *Northeast,* ed. Trigger, 760–62, 768–70.

20. Hickerson, *Chippewa and Their Neighbors,* 39–40; Warren, *History of the Ojibway People,* 116–17.

21. Hickerson, *Chippewa and Their Neighbors,* 13; Warren, *History of the Ojibway People,* xiii–xiv, 127.

22. "Census of the Indian Tribes," *WHC* 17 (1906): 247; Hickerson, *Southwestern Chippewa,* 2, 72; Warren, *History of the Ojibway People,* 83–86. On the Caribou clan, see author's interview with Ellen Bushman Olson, Grand Marais, Nov. 1, 1989, transcript and notes in author's possession.

23. Hickerson, *Southwestern Chippewa,* 65–66.

24. For the two views of Du Lhut, see "Description of Wisconsin Rivers; Accusations against Du Luth," and "Illicit Fur Trade; Participation Therein of French Soldiers; Complaints against Le Sueur"—both in *WHC* 16 (1902): 107, 174. See also Solon J. Buck, "The Story of the Grand Portage," *Minnesota History Bulletin* 5 (Feb. 1923): 15; Louise Phelps Kellogg's introduction to Daniel Greysolon, sieur Duluth, "Memoir of Duluth on the Sioux Country, 1678–1682," in *Early Narratives,* 325–28.

25. Glyndwr Williams, "Highlights in the History of the First Two Hundred Years of the Hudson's Bay Company," *The Beaver,* Autumn 1970, p. 4–9.

26. Kellogg, "French Regime," 353; Innis, *Fur Trade,* 49–50; La Vérendrye, *Journals and Letters,* 6–7. In Warren, *History of the Ojibway People,* 99n1, Edward Duffield Neill discussed the copper sample from the "river Nantaouagan," which he thought was the Ontonagon (Michigan); Nantaouagan was, however, the name for the Pigeon.

27. Thistle, *Trade Relations,* 9; Perrot, "Memoir," 230; Radisson, "Radisson's Account," 35; Innis, *Fur Trade,* 60–62.

28. Innis, *Fur Trade,* 39–40, 66–67, 91, 104–9; "Sir Guy Carleton to Lord Shelburne," Mar. 2, 1768, in CPA, *Report,* 1886, p. clxx. See also Louis-Armand de Lom d'Arce, baron de Lahontan, *New Voyages to North-America,* ed. Reuben Gold Thwaites (Chicago: A. C. McClurg & Co., 1905), 1:99–101.

29. Innis, *Fur Trade,* 59, 67, 79, 85, 87, 106–7. On La Noüe, see "Intertribal Affairs; Licenses for Fur Trade; Their Suppression," *WHC* 16 (1902): 440n1.

30. Innis, *Fur Trade,* 89–90; La Vérendrye, *Journals and Letters,* 8, 44–53.

31. La Vérendrye, *Journals and Letters,* 26.

32. Innis, *Fur Trade,* 91; La Vérendrye, *Journals and Letters,* 52, 53. See also *DCB* 3, s.v. "Gaultier de Varennes et de La Vérendrye, Pierre."

33. La Vérendrye, *Journals and Letters,* 131, 436–38.

34. La Vérendrye, *Journals and Letters,* 100–101. He frequently mentioned 600 warriors gathering at Fort St. Charles, spoke of up to 1,200 going on war parties, and said the largest village contained nine hundred cabins. Since one can assume at least four dependents (women, children, and old people) to each warrior, these figures confirm his assertion that there was a "considerable population" in the area (p. 186).

35. La Vérendrye, *Journals and Letters,* 85, 136. The post among the Dakota, Fort Beauharnois, had been established in 1727 and later abandoned; La Vérendrye was urging its reinstatement.

36. La Vérendrye, *Journals and Letters,* 175–77.

37. La Vérendrye, *Journals and Letters,* 219.

38. Hickerson, *Southwestern Chippewa,* 69–70.

39. Hickerson, *Southwestern Chippewa,* 71–72. In 1749 La Vérendrye called the newcomers at Rainy Lake "Gens de la Graisse d'Ours," or the Beargrease people. The name continued to be common in the Grand Portage band and is now memorialized in the John Beargrease Sled Dog Marathon. La Vérendrye, *Journals and Letters,* 483; Olson interview.

40. "Latest News from Western Posts," *WHC* 17 (1906): 426. The missionary was Father Claude Coquart. Mamongeseda, who became war chieftain of the Lake Superior Ojib-

way, came from the Grand Portage Caribou clan; perhaps he or his father was the un-named leader. See Warren, *History of the Ojibway People*, 218–19.

41. La Vérendrye, *Journals and Letters*, 25–26, 224, 266, 270, 283, 301; Innis, *Fur Trade*, 94–95.

42. La Vérendrye, *Journals and Letters*, 113, 448–50.

43. La Vérendrye, *Journals and Letters*, 460, 465.

44. La Vérendrye, *Journals and Letters*, 432, 451.

45. La Vérendrye, *Journals and Letters*, 486.

46. Innis, *Fur Trade*, 98, 101, 109; B. C. Payette, comp., *Old French Papers* (Montreal: Privately printed for Payette Radio, 1966), 298–302.

47. A. and N. Woolworth, "Grand Portage National Monument" 2: structure/feature no. 12; La Vérendrye, *Journals and Letters*, 38–39; W. Stewart Wallace, *The Pedlars from Quebec and Other Papers on the Nor'Westers* (Toronto: Ryerson Press, 1954), xii; Williams, "Highlights," 25.

48. La Vérendrye, *Journals and Letters*, 39; Innis, *Fur Trade*, 96–97.

49. Jacques le Gardeur, sieur de St. Pierre, "Memoir or Summary Journal," in CPA, *Report*, 1886, p. clviii–clxix, which dates St. Pierre's trip one year too early. The date given here is from "Peace among Northwestern Tribes," *WHC* 18 (1908): 133–34.

50. Kellogg, "French Regime," 357; R. McKenzie, "Reminiscences," 47; "Letter of Benjamin Frobisher to Adam Mabane, Dated Montreal, April 19, 1784," in *Documents*, ed. Wallace, 70; Wallace, *Pedlars*, 1. For more on the ship, see "Copper Mines on Lake Superior," *WHC* 17 (1906): 237n2. It was built to serve the posts and copper mines on the south shore but may have gotten to Grand Portage.

51. Wallace, *Pedlars*, 1–2; Warren, *History of the Ojibway People*, 194–95, 218–19.

## Chapter 3. Across the Divide

1. Macdonell, "Diary," 99–100.

2. On Henry's encounter with the Ojibway, here and seven paragraphs below, see his *Travels and Adventures*, v, xxiv, 3, 11, 34–39, 43–45. The spelling of the chief's name follows Warren, *History of the Ojibway People*, 199.

3. Henry, *Travels and Adventures*, 47–48; Innis, *Fur Trade*, 188; Thompson Maxwell, "Thompson Maxwell's Narrative—1760–1763," *WHC* 11 (1888): 213–15. Rogers' Rangers was a unit formed during the French and Indian War that used Indian skirmishing tactics.

4. Henry, *Travels and Adventures*, 73–104, 156–58; Warren, *History of the Ojibway People*, 204–9.

5. Henry, *Travels and Adventures*, 184, 187.

6. Innis, *Fur Trade*, 173.

7. Paolo Andriani, quoted in François-Alexandre-Frédéric, duc de La Rochefoucauld-Liancourt, "Tour through Upper Canada," ed. William Renwick Riddell, in Province of Ontario, Bureau of Archives, *Thirteenth Report*, 1916, p. 113.

8. Jonathan Carver, *The Journals of Jonathan Carver and Related Documents, 1766–1770*, ed. John Parker (St. Paul: MHS Press, 1976), 12–21, 130–31. See also Carver, *Travels through the Interior Parts of North America, in the Years 1766, 1767, and 1768* (1781; reprint, Minneapolis: Ross & Haines, 1956), 106, 131; in this version of his journals, first published in London where the Hudson's Bay Company was powerful, Carver blamed the Indians' criticisms on "the intrigues of the Canadian traders" (p. 111).

9. Here and below, see Carver, *Journals*, 131, 132, 172, 191; and *Travels*, 123. The speculation about the palisaded structure is based on John Tanner, who mentioned fortified camps built in dangerous areas, and Henry's 1775 observation that the Ojibway on the border lakes had been subject to much attack from the Dakota. See Hickerson, *Chippewa and Their Neighbors*, 94; Henry, *Travels and Adventures*, 238–39.

10. Carver, *Journals*, 132; Nancy L. Woolworth, "Grand Portage in the Revolutionary War," *MH* 44 (Summer 1975): 200; Wallace, *Pedlars*, 4–9; Innis, *Fur Trade*, 188–90.

11. Innis, *Fur Trade*, 28; Frobishers to Haldimand, in *Documents*, ed. Wallace, 70.

12. Henry, *Travels and Adventures*, 241–42, describing an incident at Lake of the Woods.

13. Henry, *Travels and Adventures*, 260. On p. 290–91 he mentioned another such ceremony, which included a "weeping-scene" similar to the one Perrot described on p. 27, above.

14. Frobishers to Haldimand, in *Documents*, ed. Wallace, 70–71; Henry, *Travels and Adventures*, 243–44; Hickerson, *Chippewa and Their Neighbors*, 79; Thistle, *Trade Relations*, 30.

15. Wallace, *Pedlars*, 9–10.

16. Henry, *Travels and Adventures*, 240; Thistle, *Trade Relations*, 28–29.

17. "Trade in the Lake Superior Country in 1778," *MPHC* 19 (1892): 337; Nute, ed., "Legal Case," 134. Nute believed the "Erskine" who cleared the site of the later North West Company post was probably John Askin of Michilimackinac; A. and N. Woolworth disputed this in "Grand Portage National Monument" 1:166. The description of the posts is based on Verchères, "Journal," 15–16.

18. "Trade," *MPHC* 19, p. 337–38; Bigsby, *Shoe and Canoe* 2:240; Henry, *Travels and Adventures*, 230, 235; Wallace, *Pedlars*, 15; A. Mackenzie, *Journals and Letters*, 70–71.

19. Frobishers to Haldimand, in *Documents*, ed. Wallace, 71, 74.

20. A. Mackenzie, *Journals and Letters*, 70–71.

21. Wallace, *Pedlars*, 9, 12, 13; Henry, *Travels and Adventures*, 253n6, 267; E. Thompson, *Grand Portage*, 21; *DCB* 4, 5, s.v. "Frobisher, Benjamin," "Frobisher, Joseph"; Harry W. Duckworth, ed., *The English River Book: A North West Company Journal and Account Book of 1786*, Rupert's Land Record Society Series (Montreal and Kingston: McGill-Queen's University Press, 1990), xiii–xiv.

22. Wallace, *Pedlars*, 21; Peter Pond, "The Narrative of Peter Pond," in *Five Fur Traders*, ed. Gates, 27–28; A. Mackenzie, *Journals and Letters*, 75–76. For more on Pond, see Henry R. Wagner, *Peter Pond, Fur Trader and Explorer*, Yale University Library Western Historical Series, no. 2 (New Haven: The Library, 1955); Harold A. Innis, *Peter Pond, Fur Trader and Adventurer* (Toronto: Irwin & Gordon, 1930).

23. A. Mackenzie, *Journals and Letters*, 73.

24. *DCB* 5, s.v. "McTavish, Simon"; Wallace, *Pedlars*, 27–28, 31–32; A. Mackenzie, *Journals and Letters*, 6–7. Innis, *Peter Pond*, 67, 75–76, suggested that McTavish was one of Pond's backers; Innis was unconvinced, however, that Pond was a party to the Henry-Frobisher coalition, as Henry implied. A forty-ton sloop was built on Lake Superior for a short-lived mining venture; it was sold in 1774, possibly to John Askin or McTavish. See Henry, *Travels and Adventures*, 220, 229.

25. Henry, *Travels and Adventures*, xxi–xxiii, 331, 334–37; *DCB* 5, s.v. "McTavish, Simon." This profitable year enabled Henry to retire to Montreal, where he became a merchant and, later, John Jacob Astor's mentor in the fur trade business.

26. For the facts, see Innis, *Fur Trade*, 176, 178–79. The interpretation is entirely the author's.

27. "Trade," *MPHC* 19, p. 337–39; N. Woolworth, "Revolutionary War," 201–3.

28. John Askin, *The John Askin Papers*, ed. Milo Milton Quaife (Detroit: Detroit Library Commission, 1928), 1:97–98, 103.

29. N. Woolworth, "Revolutionary War," 203–6.

30. "Lieutenant-Governor Hamilton to Lord Sydney," June 6, 1785, in CPA, *Report, 1890*, p. 48; "Report from Charles Grant to General Haldimand on the Fur Trade, April 24, 1780," in *Documents*, ed. Wallace, 62–66; Innis, *Fur Trade*, 181, 187; Askin, *Papers* 1:76; E. Thompson, *Grand Portage*, 28–29.

31. "Report from Grant," in *Documents*, ed. Wallace, 66; Duncan McGillivray, "Some Account of the Trade Carried on by the North West Company," in CPA, *Report, 1928*, p. 60.

32. Here and two paragraphs below, see Innis, *Fur Trade*, 215, 219–20, 242; "Benjamin Frobisher to Hon. Henry Hamilton," May 2, 1785, in CPA, *Report, 1890*, p. 55–56; La Rochefoucauld-Liancourt, "Tour," 113; A. Mackenzie, *Journals and Letters*, 81–84.

33. Innis, *Fur Trade*, 220, 225; A. Mackenzie, *Journals and Letters*, 84; Harmon, *Sixteen Years*, 211; Frobishers to Haldimand, in *Documents*, ed. Wallace, 73.

34. Frobishers to Haldimand, in *Documents*, ed. Wallace, 73.

35. Innis, *Fur Trade*, 230, 246; A. Mackenzie, *Journals and Letters*, 81.

36. Frobishers to Haldimand, in *Documents*, ed. Wallace, 74; Inglis, quoted in Innis, *Fur Trade*, 248.

37. Washington Irving, *Astoria; or, Anecdotes of an Enterprise beyond the Rocky Mountains*, ed. Edgeley W. Todd, AETS, no. 44 (Norman: University of Oklahoma Press, 1964), 11; Ross, *Fur Hunters*, 7.

38. Innis, *Fur Trade*, 214; Henry, *Travels and Adventures*, 25; A. Mackenzie, *Journals and Letters*, 436.

39. Frobishers to Haldimand, in *Documents*, ed. Wallace, 73–74; Innis, *Fur Trade*, 214, 232; McGillivray, "Some Account," 69.

40. Quoted in R. McKenzie, "Reminiscences," 33.

41. Harmon, *Sixteen Years*, 12, 27, 51, 65; A. Mackenzie, *Journals and Letters*, 453.

42. Here and below, see Harmon, *Sixteen Years*, 17, 37–38, 45, 46, 67.

43. Here and below, see Harmon, *Sixteen Years*, 43, 55, 74.

44. Here and below, see Harmon, *Sixteen Years*, 50, 56, 62–63, 98, 108, 125, 186, 194.

45. Harmon, *Sixteen Years*, 105, 109; Wentzel, "Letters," 108. Other good examples of this process are Charles MacKenzie, "The Mississouri Indians: A Narrative of Four Trading Expeditions to the Mississouri, 1804–1805–1806," in *Les Bourgeois*, ed. Masson, 1:318; and George Nelson, "Winter." An excellent description of the trader acculturation process is in Warren, *History of the Ojibway People*, 386. Alexander Mackenzie spoke negatively of it in *Journals and Letters*, 65–66, though he claimed it only happened to Frenchmen. The "poverty and obscurity" statement was applied to David Thompson, another good example of acculturation; see Wallace, *Pedlars*, 68.

## Chapter 4. The Hurly-Burly of Business

1. A. Mackenzie, *Journals and Letters*, 74.

2. Mitchell Oman, quoted by David Thompson, *Narrative*, 236.

3. Warren, *History of the Ojibway People*, 261–62; A. Mackenzie, *Journals and Letters*, 111. Though Mackenzie was ostensibly the author of the quotation, it was probably written by David Thompson, who traveled through northern Minnesota in 1798.

4. The author found no Indian accounts of the 1781–82 epidemic; this description is generally based on accounts of later ones where mortality was similar—for instance, the 1837 epidemic among the Hidatsa. On domestic violence, see, for example, Harmon, *Sixteen Years*, 61; Henry (the Younger), *Journal*, 136, 138–39, 158.

5. Warren, *History of the Ojibway People*, 260; Thistle, *Trade Relations*, 62–63; Innis, *Fur Trade*, 199.

6. Thistle, *Trade Relations*, 33, 74, 77; McGillivray, "Some Account," 62.

7. McGillivray, "Some Account," 60–61; Frobisher to Mabane, in *Documents*, ed. Wallace, 67–68.

8. Innis, *Fur Trade*, 243, 250.

9. A. Mackenzie, *Journals and Letters*, 77, 80; Marjorie Wilkins Campbell, *The North West Company* (New York: St. Martin's Press, 1957), 151–52; Innis, *Fur Trade*, 258; Irving, *Astoria*, 14; Bigsby, *Shoe and Canoe* 1:123.

10. A. Mackenzie, *Journals and Letters*, 83.

11. Here and below, see Innis, *Fur Trade*, 241; A. Mackenzie, *Journals and Letters*, 433; Ross, *Fur Hunters*, 9–11; Wentzel, "Letters," 93, 96.

12. A. Mackenzie, *Journals and Letters*, 83–84, 99; Harmon, *Sixteen Years*, 11–12; E. Thompson, *Grand Portage*, 157–59. For an example of a guide countermanding a *bourgeois*, see R. McKenzie, "Reminiscences," 9.

13. "Memorial of Montreal Merchants Respecting Trade," *MPHC* 24 (1895): 405–6; Peter Grant, "The Sauteux Indians about 1804," in *Les Bourgeois*, ed. Masson, 2:314; Irving, *Astoria*, 44.

14. A. Mackenzie, *Journals and Letters*, 424; Verchères, "Journal," 4; Johann Georg Kohl, *Kitchi-Gami: Life among the Lake Superior Ojibway*, trans. Lascelles Wraxall (1860; reprint, St. Paul: MHS Press, Borealis Books, 1985), 225; Harmon, *Sixteen Years*, 55, 67.

15. Nelson, "Winter," 232. Nelson was working for the XY Company, which operated much the same way as the North West Company.

16. Innis, *Fur Trade*, 239, 241; A. Mackenzie, *Journals and Letters*, 495.

17. A. Mackenzie, *Journals and Letters*, 83; Nute, ed., "Legal Case," 138.

18. Nute, ed., "Legal Case," 123, 125, 142.

19. Nute, ed., "Legal Case," 123–24; Campbell, *North West Company*, 155.

20. Nute, ed., "Legal Case," 140; A. Mackenzie, *Journals and Letters*, 98; Innis, *Fur Trade*, 242; McGillivray, *Journal*, 6–8. The passage from Mackenzie has two messages. Explicitly, he was denying any discontent. But in stressing how outnumbered and helpless the masters were, he betrayed their insecurity. This was clearly one autocrat to whom the idea of rebellion had occurred.

21. Frobishers to Haldimand, in *Documents*, ed. Wallace, 74; A. Woolworth, "Archaeological Excavations . . . 1970–1971," p. 69; E. Thompson, *Grand Portage*, 71, 137–40; A. Mackenzie, *Journals and Letters*, 496; Thomas Douglas, earl of Selkirk, *Lord Selkirk's Diary, 1803–1804*, ed. Patrick C. T. White, PCS, no. 35 (Toronto: Champlain Society, 1958), 214–15.

22. E. Thompson, *Grand Portage*, 53, 91–92; "Secretary [Winthrop] Sargent to the Secretary of State," Sept. 30, 1796, in U.S. Dept. of State, *The Territorial Papers of the United States* (Washington, D.C.: GPO, 1934), 2:577; A. Mackenzie, *Journals and Letters*, 492. The Quebec government had no legal right to grant land to the North West Company; Grand Portage was known to be south of the border by this date. The "point" referred to in William McGillivray's letter is thought to be a sand point just east of the mouth of Grand Portage Creek; today, only a few boulders remain of it. On the "premier's scaffold," see note 29, below.

23. Innis, *Fur Trade*, 182–83, 220–22; Grace Lee Nute, *Lake Superior*, American Lakes Series (Indianapolis: Bobbs-Merrill Co., 1944), 118; Macdonell, "Diary," 89, 94; Harmon, *Sixteen Years*, 19; A. Mackenzie, *Journals and Letters*, 475, 497; E. Thompson, *Grand Portage*, 100–101, 106.

24. R. McKenzie, "Reminiscences," 11, 66; Wallace, *Pedlars*, 52; "General Return of the Departments and Posts" and "General List of Partners, Clerks & Interpreters"—both in CPA, *Report*, 1892, p. 142, 1939, p. 53–56; E. Thompson, *Grand Portage*, 49, 101. For the blacksmith and joiner, see A. Mackenzie, *Journals and Letters*, 485, 487; the wintering spots are mentioned on p. 496. For more on Fraser (not the explorer but a Scottish relative of Simon McTavish), McKenzie, and Munro, see *Documents*, ed. Wallace, 445, 478, 488.

25. Macdonell, "Diary," 97; John McDonald of Garth, quoted in McGillivray, *Journal*, lii.

26. Here and below, see Thistle, *Trade Relations*, 16, 31, 46, 56. Harmon's diary is also replete with evidence of traders' helplessness as hunters. On post returns and food at Grand Portage, see E. Thompson, *Grand Portage*, 93, 101; A. Woolworth, "Archaeological Excavations . . . 1970–1971," p. 275–81. The post journals from Fort William frequently mention scarcity and food purchased from the Indians, and it is unlikely Grand Portage was much different.

27. R. McKenzie, "Reminiscences," 12–13. In all, the Ojibway on the border lakes sold 1,200 to 1,500 bushels of wild rice to the North West Company each year; see Harmon, *Sixteen Years*, 92.

28. Tanner, *Narrative*, 61; "Memorial," *MPHC* 24:407; A. Mackenzie, *Journals and Letters*, 491. Heriot, *Travels*, 205, stated that a canoe yard at Grand Portage produced seventy canoes a year; for a refutation, see A. and N. Woolworth, "Grand Portage National Monument" 1:137–47.

29. MHS, *The Aborigines of Minnesota: A Report*, collated by Newton H. Winchell (St. Paul: MHS, 1911), 583; Warren, *History of the Ojibway People*, 84. On Nectam, see Carver, *Journals*, 132; Macdonell, "Diary," 103; and A. Mackenzie, *Journals and Letters*, 106, who asserted that "Nectam" was a title rather than a name. William H. Keating said the scaffold was located at Fort Charlotte—evidently confusing that post with the "grand depôt of the North-west Company" on Lake Superior; see *Narrative of an Expedition to the Source of St. Peter's River, Lake Winnepeek, Lake of the Woods, &c.* (London: George B. Whittaker, 1825), 2:155–56. It may have been "the premier's scaffold" mentioned as a landmark by William McGillivray in 1799. See above, p. 71.

30. Harmon, *Sixteen Years*, 25, 193; Tanner, *Narrative*, 23–24, 26. Harmon's quotation about the Iroquois referred to an area farther west but was doubtless true of the northern Minnesota region as well.

31. "Memorial," in *MPHC* 24:404, 408.

32. William E. Lass, *Minnesota's Boundary with Canada: Its Evolution since 1783*, MHS Public Affairs Center Publications (St. Paul: MHS Press, 1980), 12–18.

33. Wallace, ed., *Documents*, 9–10, 72; "Memorial," *MPHC* 24:406.

34. Carolyn Gilman, "Grand Portage Ojibway Indians Give British Medals to Historical Society," *MH* 47 (Spring 1980): 27–28; "Memorial," *MPHC* 24:407–8.

35. A. Mackenzie, *Journals and Letters*, 77–78; Wallace, ed., *Documents*, 8.

36. A. Mackenzie, *Journals and Letters*, 9–10; Innis, *Peter Pond*, 106. The Frobishers used Pond's map in yet another effort to get a monopoly out of the British government; see "Memorial of Peter Pond," in CPA, *Report*, 1890, p. 52–54.

37. Innis, *Fur Trade*, 253. Roderick spelled his last name "McKenzie," reflecting variants that were common in other Scottish names as well.

38. A. Mackenzie, *Journals and Letters*, 2–3, 16, 24, 78, 454.

39. Bigsby, *Shoe and Canoe* 1:115 (quoting David Thompson); R. McKenzie, "Reminiscences," 11.

40. Here and two paragraphs below, see R. McKenzie, "Reminiscences," 10–12; E. Thompson, *Grand Portage*, 48–49.

41. R. McKenzie, "Reminiscences," 17–18. This passage is sometimes quoted as having happened at Grand Portage; the context makes it clear, however, that Roderick was speaking of Ile-à-la-Crosse, a post on a lake threaded by the Churchill River.

42. Wallace, *Pedlars*, 25; R. McKenzie, "Reminiscences," 18–19.

43. A. Mackenzie, *Journals and Letters*, 78–79, 430.

44. Campbell, *North West Company*, 59; A. Mackenzie, *Journals and Letters*, 432. The Mackenzie in the first quotation was probably Roderick, who was getting his information from Alexander.

45. A. Mackenzie, *Journals and Letters*, 200, 441–43.

46. Campbell, *North West Company*, 67.

47. A. Mackenzie, *Journals and Letters*, 450–52; Campbell, *North West Company*, 80.

48. A. Mackenzie, *Journals and Letters*, 453–54.

49. "Letter of Simon McTavish to Joseph Frobisher, Dated April, 1787," in *Documents*, ed. Wallace, 75–76.

50. A. Mackenzie, *Journals and Letters*, 82–83; Innis, *Fur Trade*, 258; Bigsby, *Shoe and Canoe* 1:123–24.

51. Wallace, *Pedlars*, 31–33; Campbell, *North West Company*, 117.

52. E. Thompson, *Grand Portage*, 76; Innis, *Fur Trade*, 257–58.

53. Elaine Allan Mitchell, "The North West Company Agreement of 1795," *CHR* 36 (June 1955): 131–35.

54. A. Mackenzie, *Journals and Letters*, 23–25.

55. A. Mackenzie, *Journals and Letters*, 415–16, 503.

56. Warren, *History of the Ojibway People*, 279–80, 290–94; E. Thompson, *Grand Portage*, 110.

57. This is the interpretation in Elaine Allan Mitchell, "New Evidence on the Mackenzie-McTavish Break," *CHR* 41 (Mar. 1960): 41–44. For the drinking matches, see Landmann, *Adventures and Recollections* 1:233–38, 295–96.

58. R. McKenzie, "Reminiscences," 48; Duncan McGillivray to Æneas Cameron, May 13, 1800, and McTavish to Cameron, Sept. 2, 1799—both in Mitchell, "New Evidence," 45–46. The second quotation comes from Louis R. Masson's introduction to *Les Bourgeois,* as translated by Wallace in *Pedlars,* 38. Masson may have gotten the story from Roderick, his first wife's grandfather; see also *The Macmillan Dictionary of Canadian Biography,* ed. W. Stewart Wallace, 4th ed. (Toronto: Macmillan Co. of Canada, 1978), 565.

59. William McGillivray to Æneas Cameron, May 8, 1800, in Mitchell, "New Evidence," 46.

60. Fraser to McTavish, Jan. 18, 1800, in Wallace, *Pedlars,* 40–41.

61. McTavish to the Wintering Partners, Apr. 20, 1800, quoted in *Les Bourgeois,* ed. Masson, 1:75–76; Colin Robertson, quoted in W. Stewart Wallace, "The Nor'Westers Invade the Bay," *The Beaver,* Mar. 1947, p. 33.

62. Wallace, *Pedlars,* 56–58; A. Mackenzie, *Journals and Letters,* 25; Simon McTavish to Roderick McKenzie, June 22, 1799, in R. McKenzie, "Reminiscences," 47–48. See also R. Harvey Fleming, "The Origin of 'Sir Alexander Mackenzie and Company,'" *CHR* 9 (June 1928): 137–55.

63. Harmon, *Sixteen Years,* 21.

64. A. Mackenzie, *Journals and Letters,* 36.

65. A. Mackenzie, *Journals and Letters,* 495, 499.

66. A. Mackenzie, *Journals and Letters,* 32, 495–96, 507; Nelson, "Winter," 142; Verchères, "Journal," 10–11; E. Thompson, *Grand Portage,* 105. Verchères has caused immense confusion because he said the XY fort "had been built by the Northwest Company," but from the context it is clear he meant the *New* North West Company—or XY. The fort he described could not have been the old North West Company's. Harmon, *Sixteen Years,* 20–21, stated that the original XY buildings were two hundred rods from the North West Company fort.

67. E. Thompson, *Grand Portage,* 111; Verchères, "Journal," 6–10. On the XY Company buildings at Pigeon River, see A. and N. Woolworth, "Grand Portage National Monument" 1:72–78; Wheeler et al., *Voices from the Rapids,* 39.

68. Campbell, *North West Company,* 133; François Victor Malhiot, "A Wisconsin Fur-Trader's Journal, 1804–05," *WHC* 19 (1910): 210.

69. Gordon Charles Davidson, *The North West Company* (1918; reprint, New York: Russell & Russell, 1967), 77.

70. Nelson, "Winter," 143.

71. Nelson, "Winter," 144.

72. Nelson, "Winter," 156; McDonald of Garth, "Autobiographical Notes," 25–26; Innis, *Fur Trade,* 273n35; Harmon, *Sixteen Years,* 70; Thistle, *Trade Relations,* 72. For more beatings and murder threats, see Henry (the Younger), *Journal,* 150.

73. Thistle, *Trade Relations,* 67–72; Henry (the Younger), *Journal,* 156, 158.

74. Tanner, *Narrative,* 51–52.

75. White, "'Give Us a Little Milk,'" 67, and "Skilled Game," 234–36.

76. Innis, *Fur Trade,* 235.

77. McGillivray, "Some Account," 62–63.

78. McGillivray, "Some Account," 61, 62. For traders' attitudes and comments on the effect of alcohol, see Harmon, *Sixteen Years,* 44, 73, 77; Henry (the Younger), *Journal,* 139.

79. Hickerson, *Chippewa and Their Neighbors,* 102.

80. Wallace, *Pedlars,* 30; Campbell, *North West Company,* 132, 142; "Rivalry in Northwest Trade," in *WHC* 19 (1910): 290; A. Mackenzie, *Journals and Letters,* 32, 513.

81. Wallace, ed., *Documents,* 111, 116–18, 172, 194. The first person expelled for drunkenness was Jean Baptiste Cadotte, whom Mackenzie had championed; see *Documents,* 183–84.

82. A. Mackenzie, *Journals and Letters,* 39; Campbell, *North West Company,* 143. Alexander Henry (the Elder) said that the XY Company's debts amounted to £70,000; see "Union of Northwest Companies," *WHC* 19 (1910): 310.

83. Frobisher to Mabane, in *Documents,* ed. Wallace, 69; Peter Drummond to James

Green, Sept. 9, 1797, in Peter Russell, *The Correspondence of the Honourable Peter Russell,* ed. E. A. Cruikshank and A. F. Hunter (Toronto: Ontario Historical Society, 1932), 1:276; William McGillivray to John Hale, Sept. 4, 1824, and testimonies of William Mackay and John McGillivray—all in U.S. Congress, House, *Boundary between the United States and Great Britain,* 25th Cong., 2d sess., 1838, H. Ex. Doc. 451 (Serial 331), 123, 126–27, 131; Bigsby, *Shoe and Canoe* 2:240–41.

84. D. Thompson, *Narrative,* xiv; Bigsby, *Shoe and Canoe* 1:113–14.

85. D. Thompson, *Narrative,* xxxv, lxxviii–lxxxiii, 130–31, 219; "General List," in CPA, *Report,* 1939, p. 56.

86. R. McKenzie, "Reminiscences," 46.

87. Harmon, *Sixteen Years,* 92; Innis, *Fur Trade,* 229; Bigsby, *Shoe and Canoe* 2:241; R. McKenzie, "Reminiscences," 47.

88. Nelson, "Winter," 14; McGillivray, "Some Account," 70; Franchère, *Journal,* 182; Selkirk, *Diary,* 214; Henry (the Younger), *Journal,* 144. A good summary of the sources on the move appears in A. and N. Woolworth, "Grand Portage National Monument" 1:153–59.

89. Warren, *History of the Ojibway People,* 293.

90. J[ames] Ferguson to Daniel Webster, July 25, 1842, in U.S. Congress, *Message from the President of the United States to the Two Houses of Congress,* 27th Cong., 3d sess., 1842, S. Doc. 1 (Serial 413), 105; A. Woolworth, "Archaeological Excavations . . . 1970–1971," p. 36, 47; Buck, "Story of the Grand Portage," 23–24; McDonald of Garth, "Autobiographical Notes," 34–35; David Thompson, diary, July 22, 1822, photostat in David Thompson Papers, MHS.

## Chapter 5. Roots of Community

1. The early population reports, although they agree surprisingly well, are probably underestimates; they were made by fur traders, and not all families participated in the trade. In 1809 about 150 people traded at Fort William; by 1829 that number had risen to 195, of whom 44 were from south of the border. By 1832 an American census reported 50 at Grand Portage—12 men, 11 women, and 27 children. See McGillivray, "Some Account," 66; Elizabeth Arthur, ed., *Thunder Bay District, 1821–1892: A Collection of Documents,* PCS, Ontario Series, no. 9 (Toronto: Champlain Society, 1973), 62; Henry Rowe Schoolcraft, *Schoolcraft's Expedition to Lake Itasca: The Discovery of the Source of the Mississippi,* ed. Philip P. Mason (East Lansing: Michigan State University Press, 1958), 159. Between 1874 and 1920, OIA tribal rolls list between 236 and 362 people, the numbers slowly growing as the years passed; A. and N. Woolworth, "Grand Portage National Monument" 1:200–201. The names of the chiefs are from the card index to the Fort William Journals, Old Fort William library, Thunder Bay, Ontario. These journals are dispersed among the National Archives of Canada, the Thunder Bay Historical Museum Society, and the Manitoba Provincial Archives; the card index, compiled by researchers for the reconstruction of Old Fort William, is the source for all material cited here.

2. Carver, *Journals,* 131; Arthur, ed., *Thunder Bay District,* 34, 62.

3. Warren Upham, *Minnesota Geographic Names: Their Origin and Historic Significance* (1920; reprint, St. Paul: MHS, 1969), 146; J. William Trygg, "A Study of the Tourist and Recreational Resources of the Grand Portage Indian Reservation, Minnesota," Jan. 11, 1963, p. 20, typescript in GPNM; John Fritzen, *Historic Sites and Place Names of Minnesota's North Shore* (Duluth: St. Louis County Historical Society, 1974), 25, 29.

4. Hickerson, *Southwestern Chippewa,* 82; A. Mackenzie, *Journals and Letters,* 93, 95; Harmon, *Sixteen Years,* 211; GPLCC, *Kitchi Onigaming,* 39; Densmore, *Chippewa Customs,* 124–25, 153–54; Grace Lee Nute, "The American Fur Company's Fishing Enterprises on Lake Superior," *Mississippi Valley Historical Review* 12 (Mar. 1926): 490–91.

5. Henry, *Travels and Adventures,* 55, 56–57, 66–67; GPLCC, *Kitchi Onigaming,* 19; Densmore, *Chippewa Customs,* 126.

6. Bigsby, *Shoe and Canoe* 2:202–3; Trygg, "Tourist and Recreational Resources," 11–12, exhibit A.

7. GPLCC, *Kitchi Onigaming*, 18.

8. Hickerson, *Chippewa and Their Neighbors*, 108–14, and *Southwestern Chippewa*, 14; Macdonell, "Diary," 77; A. Mackenzie, *Journals and Letters*, 96; Bigsby, *Shoe and Canoe* 2:207n.

9. Hickerson, *Southwestern Chippewa*, 4, 46–47; Thistle, *Trade Relations*, 40. Quotations are from François Clairambault d'Aigremont, in Edmund Jefferson Danziger, Jr., *The Chippewas of Lake Superior*, Civilization of the American Indian Series, vol. 148 (Norman: University of Oklahoma Press, 1978), 23, and from William Henry, in Henry, *Travels and Adventures*, viii.

10. Arthur, ed., *Thunder Bay District*, 34, 37, 64–65; Nancy L. Woolworth, "The Grand Portage Mission: 1731–1965," *MH* 39 (Winter 1965): 305; "Report of the Lake Superior District Outfit," 1829, and FWJ, Aug. 5, 1828, July 24, 1829—excerpts from both in FWJ card index.

11. Peau de Chat is frequently mentioned in the Fort William Journals, often in close proximity to Espagnol. Petickquishaung, Espagnol's stepson, married Peau de Chat's daughter; FWJ, July 1, 1824, July 29, 1826, Mar. 21, 1827. On Grand Coquin, see FWJ, Feb. 10, 1824; Bigsby, *Shoe and Canoe* 2:265. On Joseph Peau de Chat, see Arthur, ed., *Thunder Bay District*, 14. The missionary was Father Nicholas Frémiot.

12. Bigsby, *Shoe and Canoe* 2:232, 246; Francis Xavier Pierz, baptismal records, 1838–39, p. 22, photostat in Francis Pierz Papers, MHS; U.S. Laws, Statutes, etc., *Indian Affairs: Laws and Treaties*, comp. and ed. by Charles J. Kappler (Washington, D.C., 1904), 2:568, 651. The age listed for Joseph "Saganachens" in Pierz's 1839 records could be either fifty-nine or thirty-nine. The latter matches Bigsby's description better.

13. Richard F. Morse, "The Chippewas of Lake Superior," *WHC* 3 (1857; reprint, 1904): 354–55.

14. Thistle, *Trade Relations*, 40; Warren, *History of the Ojibway People*, 135, 316; Arthur, ed., *Thunder Bay District*, xlv–xlvi, 17.

15. Tanner, *Narrative*, 144–47.

16. Warren, *History of the Ojibway People*, 322–23; Tanner, *Narrative*, 147.

17. "John Kinzie to Thomas Forsyth," July 7, 1812, in U.S. Dept. of State, *Territorial Papers* 16 (1948): 249; Warren, *History of the Ojibway People*, 369–71; Danziger, *Chippewas*, 66. Ojibway activity in the War of 1812 was doubtless what prompted Lewis Cass, governor of Michigan Territory, to urge the United States in 1815 to found a post at Grand Portage for the "salutary effects" it would have "upon the minds of the Indians"; see "Wisconsin Posts Recommended," *WHC* 19 (1910): 376–79.

18. Warren, *History of the Ojibway People*, 324; Tanner, *Narrative*, 147; Gilman, "Grand Portage Ojibway Indians," 30.

19. Lass, *Minnesota's Boundary*, 1–2, 69–71; Arthur, ed., *Thunder Bay District*, xxv; Bigsby, *Shoe and Canoe* 2:266.

20. Innis, *Fur Trade*, 187; Nute, ed., "Legal Case," 120–21; N. Woolworth, "Revolutionary War," 208; Buck, "Story of the Grand Portage," 24n22; Bigsby, *Shoe and Canoe* 2:234.

21. A. Mackenzie, *Journals and Letters*, 84; Gabriel Richard to Bishop [John] Carroll, June 1799, in J. A. Girardin, "Life and Times of Rev. Gabriel Richard," *MPHC* 1 (1877): 484; "Minutes of the Meetings of the North West Company at Grand Portage and Fort William, 1801–1807," in *Documents*, ed. Wallace, 210–11; Harmon, *Sixteen Years*, 5–6; Warren, *History of the Ojibway People*, 195.

22. Duncan Cameron, "The Nipigon Country, 1804," in *Les Bourgeois*, ed. Masson, 2:296–97; Innis, *Fur Trade*, 259–62.

23. Robert MacRobb deposition, Dec. 17, 1818, in Great Britain, Colonial Office, *Papers Relating to the Red River Settlement* (London, 1819), 67–68; Keating, *Narrative* 2:138; Henry Youle Hind, *Narrative of the Canadian Red River Exploring Expedition of 1857 and of the Assinniboine and Saskatchewan Exploring Expedition of 1858* (1860; reprint, New York: Greenwood Press, 1969), 1:14, 74–76; James H. Baker, "History of Transportation in Minnesota," *Minnesota Historical Collections* 9 (1901): 9; *DCB* 5, s.v. "Douglas, Thomas";

Old Fort William, "Old Fort William at a Glance," 13–14.

24. Arthur, ed., *Thunder Bay District*, 33.

25. Thistle, *Trade Relations*, 82, 86; Warren, *History of the Ojibway People*, 385; Bigsby, *Shoe and Canoe* 1:126.

26. Thistle, *Trade Relations*, 75, 81; FWJ, June 27, 30, July 15, 21, 1827, Jan. 1, 1828, quotations from Jan. 21, 1831, Dec. 20, 1823.

27. Warren, *History of the Ojibway People*, 383; Crooks to Robert Stuart, Apr. 8, 1822, in International Joint Commission, *Final Report . . . on the Lake of the Woods Reference* (Washington, D.C.: GPO, 1917), 127; J. Ward Ruckman, "Ramsay Crooks and the Fur Trade of the Northwest," *MH* 7 (Mar. 1926): 22–23.

28. Chapman, letter book, 1823–24, p. 4, 6, 7, 15–16, 19, in Henry Hastings Sibley Papers, MHS; FWJ, Dec. 15, 17, 1823, June 6, 1824, and R. Mackenzie, "Report for Fort William District 1828/29" (excerpt in FWJ card index).

29. "Mr. [Henry Rowe] Schoolcraft's Report in Relation to the Fur Trade," Oct. 24, 1831, in U.S. Congress, Senate, *Message from the President of the United States in Compliance with a Resolution of the Senate Concerning the Fur Trade, and Inland Trade to Mexico*, 22d Cong., 1st sess., 1832, S. Doc. 90 (Serial 213), 43, 46; Alvin C. Gluek, Jr., *Minnesota and the Manifest Destiny of the Canadian Northwest: A Study in Canadian-American Relations* (Toronto: University of Toronto Press, 1965), 43. The American Fur Company's posts at Grand Portage have never been researched or found. In 1829 an Indian reported that the Americans were building at Roche de Bout, halfway between Grand Portage and Fond du Lac, but they were back at Grand Portage by the early 1830s. See FWJ, July 29, 1826, Apr. 30, 1827, Oct. 4, 1829; Schoolcraft, *Expedition*, 191.

30. Nute, "Fishing Enterprises," 485–89, 491–93; Ruckman, "Ramsay Crooks," 25.

31. Here and below, see Nute, "Fishing Enterprises," 489–91, 493; Gabriel Franchère, "Remarks made on a visit from Lapointe to the Fishing Stations of Grand Portage, Isle Royal and Ance Quiwinan," Aug. 1839, p. 1–3, typescript transcription in Gabriel Franchère Papers, MHS. Douglass Houghton visited Grand Portage in 1840. His field notes locate the American Fur Company's fishing station east of Grand Portage Creek. Arthur, ed., *Thunder Bay District*, 43; Bernard C. Peters (Northern Michigan University) to Alan Woolworth (MHS), July 26, 1990, Jan. 8, 1991.

32. Franchère, "Remarks," 2; Arthur, ed., *Thunder Bay District*, xxvi, 9–10, 43; FWJ, Aug. 22, 1837.

33. Nute, "Fishing Enterprises," 495–501.

34. N. Woolworth, "Grand Portage Mission," 303–4.

35. Paul Buffalo, quoted in Timothy G. Roufs, "Nature and the Concept of Power among Mississippi and Lake Superior Ojibwa: Reflections of Paul Buffalo," June 1978, p. 6–8, 10–11, typescript in GPNM.

36. George Nelson, *"The Orders of the Dreamed": George Nelson on Cree and Northern Ojibwa Religion and Myth, 1823*, ed. Jennifer S. H. Brown and Robert Brightman, Manitoba Studies in Native History, no. 3 (St. Paul: MHS Press; Winnipeg: University of Manitoba Press, 1988), 138–46; GPLCC, *Kitchi Onigaming*, 63; Roufs, "Nature and the Concept of Power," 15. The first source refers to the Cree but reflects Ojibway beliefs as well. See also Basil Johnston, *Ojibway Heritage* (New York: Columbia University Press, 1976).

37. W. J. Hoffman, "The Mide'wiwin or 'Grand Medicine Society' of the Ojibwa," in U.S. Bureau of Ethnology, *Seventh Annual Report* (Washington, D.C.: GPO, 1891), 156–59; Hickerson, *Chippewa and Their Neighbors*, 52–56; Nancy Way Lienke, "Ethnomethodology in a Chippewa Community Using Above-Ground Artifacts in a Free Association Technique," n.d., p. 47, typescript in GPNM.

38. Here and six paragraphs below, see N. Woolworth, "Grand Portage Mission," 304–10; Arthur, ed., *Thunder Bay District*, 73. Espagnol's wife was baptized Josette Otakakwan; Pierz's baptismal records, p. 22, list her as being sixty, not seventy; Pierz Papers, MHS.

## Chapter 6. The Boundary of Cultures

1. Warren, *History of the Ojibway People,* 117, 118.

2. Arthur, ed., *Thunder Bay District,* 11, 16, 18; A. and N. Woolworth, "Grand Portage National Monument" 1:189.

3. Morse, "Chippewas of Lake Superior," 355; U.S. Laws, *Indian Affairs* 2:648–51.

4. A. and N. Woolworth, "Grand Portage National Monument" 1:190; U.S. Laws, *Indian Affairs* 2:649. For the acreage see, for example, OIA, *Report,* 1880, p. 173; on the satellite settlements, see Willis H. Raff, *Pioneers in the Wilderness: Minnesota's Cook County, Grand Marais and the Gunflint in the Nineteenth Century* (Grand Marais, Minn.: Cook County Historical Society, 1981), 52.

5. A. and N. Woolworth, "Grand Portage National Monument" 1:191, 2: structure/feature no. 54; Alexander McDougall, *The Autobiography of Captain Alexander McDougall* ([Duluth?]: A. Miller McDougall & Lewis G. Castle, 1932), 35. On Elliott and Drouillard, see Raff, *Pioneers,* 7; U.S. Dept. of State, *Register of Officers and Agents . . . in the Service of the United States . . . 1859* (Washington, D.C.: William A. Harris, 1859), 90; U.S. Dept. of the Interior, *Register of Officers and Agents . . . 1861* (Washington, D.C.: GPO, 1862), 84; OIA, *Report,* 1858, p. 47–48.

6. U.S. Dept. of the Interior, *Register . . . 1861,* p. 84; OIA, *Report,* 1857, p. 32–34, 1858, p. 48.

7. OIA, *Report,* 1856, p. 32–33, 1858, p. 47, 1860, p. 52; MHS, *Aborigines,* 657; A. and N. Woolworth, "Grand Portage National Monument" 1:190–92. The last contains a useful summary of the OIA reports for 1855–1909; see p. 190–99.

8. Isaac L. Mahan, "Grand Portage Bands, Northern Minn.," and "Lake Superior Agency," in *American Missionary* (American Missionary Association) 19, 20 (Nov. 1875, Nov. 1876): 251–52, 250–52; A. and N. Woolworth, "Grand Portage National Monument" 1:193.

9. Raff, *Pioneers,* 5, 6, 14; Hind, *Narrative* 1:74–75. The Hudson's Bay Company complained that McCullough's traders made expeditions across the border to Lake Nipigon and Pays Plat; see Arthur, ed., *Thunder Bay District,* 103.

10. Here and below, see Mary L. Emmons to Solon J. Buck, Nov. 2, 1927, and Newton J. Bray to Grace Lee Nute, Jan. 31, 1931—both letters in Minnesota History Information File, MHS Archives, MHS; Paul LaPlante, "Statement of Paul LaPlante made at Grand Portage," Apr. 20, 1931, typescript in MHS.

11. Raff, *Pioneers,* 4, 131, 135, 158, 191; Bigsby, *Shoe and Canoe* 2:192n, 193–94; Trygg, "Tourist and Recreational Resources," 10–11; Silver Mountain Mining and Milling Company, Minneapolis, *Prospectus . . .; Property Located in Thunder Bay District, Ontario, Canada* ([Minneapolis, 1892?]), 13, 17. The copper mine on Susie Island was a one-season enterprise of the Falconer family, backed by some Iowa investors; see Dewey Albinson, "A Grand Portage Story and Some Other Tales from the North Country," 1963, p. 90, typescript in MHS; *Duluth News-Tribune,* Mar. 14, 1939, p. 1.

12. Here and two paragraphs below, see Elinor Barr, "Lumbering in the Pigeon River Watershed," *Papers and Records* (Thunder Bay Historical Museum Society) 4 (1976): 3–9; Raff, *Pioneers,* 51, 105–7, 117; *R. L. Polk & Co.'s Duluth Directory, 1900,* p. 91.

13. U.S. Congress, House, *Chippewa Indians in Minnesota,* 51st Cong., 1st sess., 1890, H. Ex. Doc. 247 (Serial 2747), 25, 178–79; Jay P. Kinney, "Memorandum regarding requested extension of time on Corcoran & Johnson timber contracts, Grand Portage Reservation, Minnesota," Mar. 31, 1926, in Jay P. Kinney Papers, MHS. Kinney believed that the reservation had been logged before 1900, then again starting in 1907; however, the timber had not been sold by 1898. See A. and N. Woolworth, "Grand Portage National Monument" 1:197–98. In U.S. Congress, Senate, Committee on Indian Affairs, *Survey of Conditions of the Indians in the United States,* part 39 (Washington, D.C.: GPO, 1942), 22498, it is stated that logging on tribal, allotted, and ceded lands started as early as 1904.

14. Raff, *Pioneers,* 42; U.S. Congress, House, *Chippewa Indians,* 23; Nancy L. Woolworth, "Miss Densmore Meets the Ojibwe: Frances Densmore's Ethnomusicology Stud-

ies among the Grand Portage Ojibwe in 1905," *Minnesota Archaeologist* 38 (Aug. 1979): 109; James Hull, *Red Shadows in the Mist* ([Grand Portage, Minn.]: Privately published, 1969), 14; *Cook County News-Herald* (Grand Marais), June 20, 1935, p. 1, 4; *Polk & Co.'s Duluth Directory, 1900*, p. 132.

15. OIA, *Report*, 1882, p. 176; Raff, *Pioneers*, 52, 57–58; Olson interview. By 1896 about half the band lived at Grand Marais; see A. and N. Woolworth, "Grand Portage National Monument" 1:197.

16. Here and below, see Raff, *Pioneers*, 292–303.

17. Raff, *Pioneers*, 9, 14–15, 46, 47, 65–66.

18. U.S. Congress, House, *Chippewa Indians*, 23, 59–60, 178–79; GPLCC, *Kitchi Onigaming*, 53–54; A. and N. Woolworth, "Grand Portage National Monument" 1:197.

19. MHS, *Aborigines*, 697.

20. Here and below, see N. Woolworth, "Miss Densmore," 107–8, 110; Charles Hofmann, comp. and ed., *Frances Densmore and American Indian Music: A Memorial Volume*, Contributions from the Museum of the American Indian, Heye Foundation, vol. 23 (New York: The Foundation, 1968), 25–26. On Caribou and Shingibis, see "Census Roll of the Grand Portage Chippeway Indians," Oct. 24, 1889, typescript transcription by Nancy Way Lienke in GPNM; *Cook County News-Herald*, Aug. 18, 1921, p. 5; Raff, *Pioneers*, 56.

21. The name Maymushkowaush is mentioned in the 1889 census as well as in the Fort William Journals and Pierz's 1838–39 baptismal records. Densmore's field notes associate the name Louis Gabiosa with one of the British medals. I have been unable to identify him.

22. Here and below, see N. Woolworth, "Miss Densmore," 107, 110–13; Hofmann, comp. and ed., *Frances Densmore*, 27–28.

23. Here and below, see Albinson, "Grand Portage Story," 2, 4, 5, 6.

24. Here and below, see Albinson, "Grand Portage Story," 7–9, 39.

25. Albinson, "Grand Portage Story," 8–9.

26. A. and N. Woolworth, "Grand Portage National Monument" 1:197–98; Olson interview; Albinson, "Grand Portage Story," 11–12, 35; Gilman, "Grand Portage Ojibway Indians," 31.

27. Albinson, "Grand Portage Story," 11; Lienke, "Ethnomethodology," 58, 59; Olson interview; Trygg, "Tourist and Recreational Resources," 18–19.

28. Here and below, see George M. Schwartz, *A Guidebook to Minnesota Trunk Highway No. 1*, Minnesota Geological Survey, Bulletin no. 20 (Minneapolis: University of Minnesota, 1925), 87–88; Lloyd Hendrickson interview with Gordon Lindemann, Grand Portage, Apr. 16, 1980, transcript in Cook County Historical Society File, Grand Marais Public Library, Grand Marais, Minn.; Albinson, "Grand Portage Story," 66; *Cook County News-Herald*, June 20, 1935, p. 1, 4, July 12, 1951, p. 1; A. and N. Woolworth, "Grand Portage National Monument" 1:219. The Isle Royale trips were later taken over by Roy Oberg and the Sivertson family.

29. Danziger, *Chippewas*, 131–33; David Beaulieu, "A Place Among Nations: Experiences of Indian People," in *Minnesota in a Century of Change: The State and Its People Since 1900*, ed. Clifford E. Clark, Jr. (St. Paul: Minnesota Historical Society Press, 1989), 415.

30. GPLCC, *Kitchi Onigaming*, 59, 66; U.S. Laws, *Indian Affairs* (Washington, D.C., 1979), 7:1421–22; Elizabeth Ebbott, *Indians in Minnesota*, 4th ed. (Minneapolis: University of Minnesota Press and League of Women Voters of Minnesota, 1985), 25.

31. GPLCC, *Kitchi Onigaming*, 61–62; U.S. Congress, Senate, *Survey*, 22473–74; Albinson, "Grand Portage Story," 38.

32. Albinson, "Grand Portage Story," 39.

33. Here and below, see R. Newell Searle, *Saving Quetico-Superior: A Land Set Apart* (St. Paul: MHS Press, 1977), 138–39; Albinson, "Grand Portage Story," 41–45, 64, 95, 112, 114; U.S. Congress, Senate, *Survey*, 22411–12, 22422, 22461.

34. Here and below, see U.S. Congress, Senate, *Survey*, 22473–74, 22496–505; Les Miller, "North Shore Highway Completed," *Minnesota Highways* (Minn. Dept. of Highways), Oct. 1966, p. 7.

35. Here and below, see Buck, "Story of the Grand Portage," 27.

36. Schwartz, *Guidebook*, 88; Albinson, "Grand Portage Story," 19–22.

37. Ron Cockrell, "Grand Portage National Monument, Minnesota: An Administrative History" (Omaha: NPS, Midwest Regional Office, Oct. 1983), 12.

38. Cockrell, "Grand Portage National Monument," 14–15; Calvin W. Gower, "The CCC Indian Division: Aid for Depressed Americans, 1933–1942," *MH* 43 (Spring 1972): 7, 11–12.

39. Here and below, see Ralph D. Brown, "Archaeological Investigation of the Northwest Company's Post, Grand Portage, Minnesota, 1936," *Indians at Work* (OIA), May 1937, p. 38–43; Willoughby M. Babcock, "Grand Portage Rises Again," *The Beaver,* Sept. 1941, p. 55. Brown never wrote a report on his excavations. In 1963 Alan R. Woolworth assembled all the remaining records in his typescript report "Archeological Excavations at the North West Company's Fur Trade Depot, Grand Portage, Minnesota, in 1936–1937 by the Minnesota Historical Society"; see p. 50, 53, 57, 111–13, 132–71.

40. Here and below, see Cockrell, "Grand Portage National Monument," 15–16, 28–30, 33.

41. Cockrell, "Grand Portage National Monument," 35–37.

42. Here and two paragraphs below, see A. and N. Woolworth, "Grand Portage National Monument" 1:230–55; A. Woolworth, "Archaeological Excavations . . . 1970–1971," p. 53–54, 56–58, 90–91, 276–82.

43. Wheeler et al., *Voices from the Rapids,* 39–44, 85–93.

44. Hull, *Red Shadows,* 57.

45. *Cook County News-Herald,* July 17, 1969, p. 1; Cockrell, "Grand Portage National Monument," 47–51, 60.

46. Here and below, see *Duluth News-Tribune,* May 1, 1969, p. 1; GPLCC, *Kitchi Onigaming,* 70–72; *Minneapolis Tribune,* May 1, 1975, p. 1B–2B. The Hilton hotel chain was the band's first partner on the lodge project but backed out. On forest management, see U.S. Bureau of Indian Affairs, Minneapolis Area Office, "Grand Portage Forest Resources Management Plan and Environmental Assessment," Aug. 1986.

47. Lienke, "Ethnomethodology," 55–56. The interviews were done in 1962, but the same attitudes are expressed today.

48. Hull, *Red Shadows,* 5.

# Suggested Reading

Bigsby, John J. *The Shoe and Canoe; or, Pictures of Travel in the Canadas.* 2 vols. London: Chapman & Hall, 1850.

Buck, Solon J. "The Story of the Grand Portage." *Minnesota History Bulletin* 5 (Feb. 1923): 14–27.

Campbell, Marjorie Wilkins. *The North West Company.* New York: St. Martin's Press, 1957.

Carver, Jonathan. *The Journals of Jonathan Carver and Related Documents, 1766–1770.* Ed. John Parker. St. Paul: Minnesota Historical Society (MHS) Press, 1976.

Delafield, Joseph. *The Unfortified Boundary.* Ed. Robert McElroy and Thomas Riggs. New York: Privately published, 1943.

Densmore, Frances. *Chippewa Customs.* 1929. Reprint. St. Paul: MHS Press, Borealis Books, 1979.

Ebbott, Elizabeth. *Indians in Minnesota.* 4th ed. Minneapolis: University of Minnesota Press and League of Women Voters of Minnesota, 1985.

Gates, Charles M., ed. *Five Fur Traders of the Northwest.* St. Paul: MHS, 1965.

Grand Portage Local Curriculum Committee. *A History of Kitchi Onigaming: Grand Portage and Its People.* Cass Lake, Minn.: Minnesota Chippewa Tribe, 1983.

Harmon, Daniel Williams. *Sixteen Years in the Indian Country: The Journal of Daniel Williams Harmon, 1800–1816.* Ed. W. Kaye Lamb. Toronto: Macmillan Co. of Canada, 1957.

Henry, Alexander, the Elder. *Travels and Adventures in Canada and the Indian Territories between the Years 1760 and 1776.* Ed. James Bain. Boston: Little, Brown, 1901.

Henry, Alexander, the Younger. *The Journal of Alexander Henry the Younger, 1799–1814.* Ed. Barry M. Gough. 2 vols. Publications of the Champlain Society, no. 56. Toronto: Champlain Society, 1988.

Hickerson, Harold. *The Chippewa and Their Neighbors: A Study in Ethnohistory.* Rev. and expanded ed. Prospect Heights, Ill.: Waveland Press, 1988.

_____. *The Southwestern Chippewa: An Ethnohistorical Study.* American Anthropological Association, Memoir 92. Menasha, Wis., 1962.

Hull, James. *Red Shadows in the Mist.* [Grand Portage, Minn.]: Privately published, 1969.

Innis, Harold A. *The Fur Trade in Canada: An Introduction to Canadian Economic History*. Rev. ed. Toronto: University of Toronto Press, 1956.

Irving, Washington. *Astoria; or, Anecdotes of an Enterprise beyond the Rocky Mountains*. Ed. Edgeley W. Todd. American Exploration and Travel Series, no. 44. Norman: University of Oklahoma Press, 1964.

Johnston, Basil. *Ojibway Heritage*. New York: Columbia University Press, 1976.

Judd, Carol M., and Arthur J. Ray, eds. *Old Trails and New Directions: Papers of the Third North American Fur Trade Conference*. Toronto: University of Toronto Press, 1980.

Keating, William H. *Narrative of an Expedition to the Source of St. Peter's River, Lake Winnepeek, Lake of the Woods, &c.* 2 vols. London: George B. Whittaker, 1825.

Kellogg, Louise Phelps. *The French Régime in Wisconsin and the Northwest*. Madison: State Historical Society of Wisconsin, 1925.

_____ , ed. *Early Narratives of the Northwest, 1634–1699*. Original Narratives of Early American History. New York: Charles Scribner's Sons, 1917.

Kohl, Johann Georg. *Kitchi-Gami: Life among the Lake Superior Ojibway*. Trans. Lascelles Wraxall. 1860. Reprint. St. Paul: MHS Press, Borealis Books, 1985.

Lahontan, Louis Armand de Lom d'Arce, baron de. *New Voyages to North-America*. Ed. Reuben Gold Thwaites. 2 vols. Chicago: A. C. McClurg & Co., 1905.

Landmann, George Thomas. *Adventures and Recollections of Colonel Landmann*. 2 vols. London: Colburn & Co., 1852.

Lass, William E. *Minnesota's Boundary with Canada: Its Evolution since 1783*. MHS Public Affairs Center Publications. St. Paul: MHS Press, 1980.

LaVérendrye, Pierre Gaultier de Varennes, sieur de. *Journals and Letters of Pierre Gaultier de Varennes de la Vérendrye and His Sons*. Ed. Lawrence J. Burpee. Publications of the Champlain Society, no. 16. Toronto: Champlain Society, 1927.

McGillivray, Duncan. *The Journal of Duncan M'Gillivray of the North West Company at Fort George on the Saskatchewan, 1794–5*. Ed. Arthur S. Morton. Toronto: Macmillan Co. of Canada, 1929.

Mackenzie, Alexander. *The Journals and Letters of Sir Alexander Mackenzie*. Ed. W. Kaye Lamb. Cambridge: Cambridge University Press, 1970.

Masson, Louis R., ed. *Les Bourgeois de la Compagnie du Nord-Ouest*. 1889–90. Reprint. 2 vols. New York: Antiquarian Press, 1960.

Minnesota Historical Society. *The Aborigines of Minnesota: A Report*. Collated by Newton H. Winchell. St. Paul: MHS, 1911.

Morriseau, Norval. *Legends of My People, the Great Ojibway*. Ed. Selwyn Dewdney. Toronto: Ryerson Press, 1965.

Nelson, George. "A Winter in the St. Croix Valley, 1802–03." Ed. Richard Bardon and Grace Lee Nute. *Minnesota History* 28 (Mar., June, Sept. 1947): 1–14, 142–59, 225–40.

Nute, Grace Lee. *Lake Superior*. American Lakes Series. Indianapolis: Bobbs-Merrill Co., 1944.

_____ . *The Voyageur's Highway*. St. Paul: MHS, 1951.

Perrot, Nicolas. "Memoir on the Manners, Customs, and Religion of the Savages of North America." In *The Indian Tribes of the Upper Mississippi Valley and Region of the Great Lakes*, trans. and ed. Emma Helen Blair, 1:25–272. Cleveland: Arthur H. Clark Co., 1911.

Raff, Willis H. *Pioneers in the Wilderness: Minnesota's Cook County, Grand Marais and the Gunflint in the Nineteenth Century*. Grand Marais, Minn.: Cook County Historical Society, 1981.

Ross, Alexander. *The Fur Hunters of the Far West*. Ed. Kenneth A. Spaulding. American Exploration and Travel Series, no. 20. Norman: University of Oklahoma Press, 1956.

Schoolcraft, Henry Rowe. *Schoolcraft's Expedition to Lake Itasca: The Discovery of the Source of the Mississippi*. Ed. Philip P. Mason. East Lansing: Michigan State University Press, 1958.

Selkirk, Thomas Douglas, earl of. *Lord Selkirk's Diary, 1803–1804*. Ed. Patrick C. T. White. Publications of the Champlain Society, no. 35. Toronto: Champlain Society, 1958.

Tanner, John. *A Narrative of the Captivity and Adventures of John Tanner*. 1830. Reprint. Minneapolis: Ross & Haines, 1956.

Thistle, Paul C. *Indian-European Trade Relations in the Lower Saskatchewan River Region to 1840*. Manitoba Studies in Native History, no. 2. Winnipeg: University of Manitoba Press, 1986.

Thompson, David. *David Thompson's Narrative, 1784–1812*. Ed. Richard Glover. Publications of the Champlain Society, no. 40. Toronto: Champlain Society, 1962.

Thompson, Erwin N. *Grand Portage: A History of the Sites, People, and Fur Trade*. Washington, D.C.: National Park Service, Office of Archeology and Historic Preservation, Division of History, 1969.

Trigger, Bruce G., ed. *Northeast*. Vol. 15 in *Handbook of North American Indians*, ed. William C. Sturtevant. Washington, D.C.: Smithsonian Institution, 1978.

Trigger, Bruce G., Toby Morantz, and Louise Dechne, eds. *"Le Castor Fait Tout": Selected Papers of the Fifth North American Fur Trade Conference, 1985*. Montreal: Lake St. Louis Historical Society, 1987.

Verchères de Boucherville, René Thomas. "Journal of Thomas Verchères de Boucherville." In *War on the Detroit*, ed. Milo Milton Quaife, 3–178. Lakeside Classics, no. 38. Chicago: Lakeside Press, 1940.

Wallace, W. Stewart. *The Pedlars from Quebec and Other Papers on the Nor'Westers*. Toronto: Ryerson Press, 1954.

_____, ed. *Documents Relating to the North West Company*. Publications of the Champlain Society, no. 22. Toronto: Champlain Society, 1934.

Warren, William W. *History of the Ojibway People*. 1885. Reprint. St. Paul: MHS Press, Borealis Books, 1984.

Wheeler, Robert C., et al. *Voices from the Rapids: An Underwater Search for Fur Trade Artifacts, 1960–73*. Minnesota Historical Archaeology Series, no. 3. St. Paul: MHS, 1975.

# Index

## PICTURE CREDITS

*Photographs and other illustrations used in this book appear through the courtesy of the institutions or persons listed below. The name of the photographer or artist, when known, is given in parentheses, as is additional information about the source of the item.*

Front cover (Virginia Danfelt), pages 6, 13 *top,* 16, 17 (Curtis L. Roy), 64, 133 and back cover, back cover (overlook, beadwork)—National Park Service, Grand Portage National Monument, Grand Portage, Minn.
Pages 2, 134, 135—Richard J. Novitsky, photographer
Page 3 *top* (Norval Morriseau, from his *Legends of My People, the Great Ojibway* [Toronto: Ryerson Press, 1965])—McGraw-Hill Ryerson Ltd., Whitby, Ontario
Page 7—Charles W. Nelson, photographer
Pages 9, 67, back cover (voyageurs)— © Will Goddard, photographer
Pages 12 (Jet Lowe, HABS MN-76-3), 78 *bottom* (Jet Lowe, HABS MN-76-4)—Historic American Buildings Survey/Historic American Engineering Record, National Park Service; negatives at the Library of Congress, Washington, D.C.
Pages 13 *bottom* (Ralph D. Brown); 14 *top;* 14 *middle,* 41, 48 *bottom,* 56 (all by Peter Latner); 14 *bottom,* 48 *top* (both by Eric Mortenson); 20 (George Heriot, from his *Travels through the Canadas* [London: Richard Phillips, 1807]); 28, 29 (Louis Armand de Lom d'Arce, baron de Lahontan, *New Voyages to North-America,* ed. Reuben Gold Thwaites, vol. 1 [Chicago: A. C. McClurg & Co., 1905]); 31 (Denis Diderot, *Encyclopédie, ou Dictionnaire Raisonné des Sciences, des Arts et des Métiers: Recueil de Planches,* vol. 3 [Paris, 1765]); 34; 36 (Minnesota Geological and Natural History Survey, *The Geology of Minnesota. Vol. I of the Final Report* [Minneapolis: Johnson, Smith & Harrison, 1884]); 39; 47; 49 (George M. Ryan for the *Minneapolis Tribune*); 70 (Abby Fuller Abbe); 76; 114; 115, 119, 120, 121 (all by Frances Densmore); 123; 124 (Dewey Albinson); 129; 131 (Alan Ominsky); 132—Minnesota Historical Society, St. Paul
Page 21 (Paul Kane; ROM 946.15.32)—Royal Ontario Museum, Toronto
Page 26 (detail from *Novae Franciae Accurata Delineatio, 1657,* map attributed to Francesco Bressani)—Canadian Association of Geographers, Montreal, Quebec
Pages 44 (C-103612), 78 *top* (Martin Archer Shee; C-167), 83 (C-164), 91 (C-18834)—National Archives of Canada, Ottawa, Ontario
Page 45 (Peter Rindisbacher, *Captain W. Andrew Bulger Saying Farewell at Fort Mackay, Prairie du Chien, Wisconsin, 1815,* ca. 1823, watercolor and ink wash on paper, 1968.262)—Amon Carter Museum, Fort Worth, Tex.
Pages 52, 93, 96, 97, 98 (all by Eastman Johnson); 111, 118 (both by George A. Newton)—St. Louis County Historical Society, Duluth, Minn.
Page 57 (Karl Kuttruff)—Mackinac Island State Park Commission, Mackinac Island, Mich.
Page 61 (William Tefft Schwarz)—The Bennington Museum, Bennington, Vt.
Page 82 (Thomas Lawrence; 8000)—National Gallery of Canada, Ottawa, Ontario
Page 101—Hudson's Bay Co., Winnipeg, Manitoba
Page 102 (attributed to Lord Selkirk; Selkirk Papers, SM, F 481, in MU 3279)—Archives of Ontario, Toronto
Page 106—St. Benedict's Convent Archives, St. Joseph, Minn.
Page 117 (B. F. Childs; negative 39908)—International Museum of Photography at George Eastman House, Rochester, N.Y.